Cuisine Courante

Cuisine Courante

BRUNO LOUBET

Text in association with Norma MacMillan

PAVILION

First published in Great Britain in 1991 by
PAVILION BOOKS LIMITED
196 Shaftesbury Avenue, London WC2H 8JL

A CIP catalogue record for this book is
available from the British Library

ISBN 1 85145 652 X

10 9 8 7 6 5 4 3 2 1

Typeset by DP Photosetting, Aylesbury, Bucks
Printed and bound in Italy
by Graphicom

CONTENTS

INTRODUCTION

AS far back as I can remember, I wanted to be a chef. I was always interested in food as a child, and ate everything. I was very fat! We had a large vegetable garden at home and some poultry, and it was my job to look after these. I used to spend at least two hours every day working in the garden and with the poultry, and I learned a lot from it. When the lovely vegetables and poultry arrived on our table, 'you can't imagine how proud I was. I think this is one of the major reasons why I have so much respect for food.

I was born and brought up in Libourne, which is a small town between St Emilion and Pomerol in the southwest of France – what we call 'Le Grand Sud'ouest'. My father's family were farmers in the area, and I have many aunts, uncles and cousins still living there (in fact, all but one of my brothers and four sisters have stayed in Bordeaux). My father had to work hard to keep all of us, and so that we could have a month's holiday every summer, he did two jobs at the same time – one for the French railway and the other for a rich wine-maker, working in the vineyards and the gardens. We children, too, worked in the vineyards. As a boy of 7, I started picking grapes and carrying baskets for 1 franc a day.

During the *vendange*, when the grapes were picked, the wine-maker liked to impress his workers with how rich and generous he was, so he put on a great feast and we all ate very well. My family also had a huge feast every year at my grandparents' farm, when the pigs were killed at the beginning of winter. My father would make the black pudding (which was then cooked in a soup we called *zimbura*), my uncles the hams, and my mother and aunts the *farces* for pâtés and the andouillettes. And my grandmother would run the whole show like a general. When we sat down to eat, there could be 50 or more of us at the long tables under the lime trees.

At other times of the year, when the family finances weren't too good, I can remember going to bed and dreaming about roast poultry, meat stew and charcuterie appearing with the wave of a magic wand. Looking back today, I am sure that this helped me to appreciate and recognise the flavours of simple, honest cooking.

School was not my cup of tea, and seeing my parents working so hard, I decided to support myself. So making what seemed an obvious choice, I went to the catering school in Bordeaux at age 14. To pay all my expenses, I worked every weekend and holiday in a restaurant as a waiter.

After 3 years, I passed my diploma, and started my first job in the kitchen of a small restaurant in the southwest. It was then that I bought a book that had a great effect on me. It was *Cuisine Minceur* by Michel Guérard. I read this book and read it again, asking myself why I had just spent 3 years in catering school learning about soft-boiled eggs on spinach with Béchamel sauce! I quickly understood that cooking needs not only energy and understanding, but a personal touch as well, that comes from the heart, and opens the doors to freedom. A further book by Michael Guérard, *Cuisine Gourmande*, strengthened my views on 'cooking as you feel'.

I moved to Brussels, to work as *chef-saucier* at the Hyatt-Regency Hotel, and then to Paris to the Michelin-starred Le Copenhague. My year there still inspires some Scandinavian touches in my cooking today, such as hot smoked salmon.

Then I was called up to do my national service, in the Navy. I was head chef for the Admiral's table. For many, national service was a waste of time, but I learnt a lot from producing food for large and important receptions as well as the many private receptions hosted by the senior officers.

After I was discharged, I applied for a job with various Michelin-starred restaurants. My only favourable answer came from La Tante Claire in London, and so in 1982 I began work there. Unfortunately, it was only a brief stay, but my sojourn at Gastronome One in Fulham was longer and much happier, and in 1985, The Good Food Guide voted me the 'Young Chef of the Year'!

The next year, I met Raymond Blanc at his superb Manoir aux Quat'Saisons. We had a long talk about our passions for food and cooking and, after about 2 hours, he asked me if I would like to work for him at Le Manoir. It was such a shock that I requested 2 weeks to think about it.

After deliberating, I accepted his offer. A year in the kitchen at Le Manoir proved to me that Raymond Blanc is one of the rare chefs to be honest with himself, with such a passion about his work as well as respect and conviviality for his customers. If something is not 100 percent up to his standard, it will be thrown in the bin and all will be started again. He will not compromise.

In September 1986, Raymond entrusted me with the job of head chef/manager of his restaurant Le Petit Blanc in Oxford where, over the course of 2 happy and successful years, I started to develop my own style of cooking, reworking classic dishes – particularly those from my native Bordeaux – to make them more modern but still keeping things simple and full of intense flavours. Raymond Blanc challenged me to think twice and so avoid the mistake of routine.

I believe that you must bring something to a dish to enhance the flavour, but if your approach is too complicated you will disguise its intrinsic qualities. I try to use the least number of ingredients because if food is too clever and sophisticated, the palate is confused.

My cooking is very honest – some may call it characterful, others may say it is hearty and earthy. Many chefs work according to the fashions and for the celebrities, never cooking the dishes they would like to eat themselves. I cook what I like, not what is regarded as fashionable.

Since March 1989, I have been Chef de Cuisine at the Four Seasons Restaurant at the Inn on the Park Hotel in London, and am very proud to have now achieved my first Michelin star. I feel I have been very lucky to have reached this stage.

Chefs work very hard – on a normal day, it's 9am to 3.30pm, then 6.30pm to midnight, and if we have a lot of people, or a banquet, or a new menu, it can run to 18 hours or so. The atmosphere in some restaurant kitchens can be tense and angry, under such pressure, but I believe strongly that the chefs who work for me, my *brigade*, should be praised for their achievements, as well as criticised for their mistakes. I take care not to lose my temper because I think that a cook who is happy will produce work three times as good as one who is unhappy. I think this is why so many chefs stay in my kitchen – which is a demanding one – for 2 years or more.

You pay a high price to succeed in this profession – like an athlete running in the Olympics, you have to give everything, and still this does not always win you a place on the podium.

I personally cannot see myself doing anything else. Cooking and my wife are my two best friends, and I hope I will keep them for life.

A LESSON IN TASTE

In the summer of 1984, my wife's grandparents invited us to have dinner with them at Alain Chapel's restaurant at Mionnay, near Lyon. The meal, service and atmosphere were a feast.

My first course had the most exciting flavours I had ever tasted: *Mille feuilles de crêtes et rognons de coq, écrevisses pattes rouges aux mousserons et jus de cerfeuil.* This dish was such a revelation to me that today, nearly seven years later, I can still remember every detail of its conception and flavours.

This dish had such an impact on my palate and my professional life that I would choose it as my last supper. And if God does not let me into Paradise, it would not matter so much now that I have had a taste of Paradise in this world.

BRUNO LOUBET,
1990

INGREDIENTS AND TECHNIQUES

CUISINE NOUVELLE uses expensive ingredients, in small quantities, but I believe a good chef or cook should be able to take any produce and make it interesting. At The Four Seasons, I have the most expensive products available from all over the world; what I like to do is to mix them with what could be called 'poor' ingredients. In fact, I prefer to use cheaper cuts of meat in my cooking – knuckle or shank of veal or neck fillet of lamb – rather than those considered to be the best.

The recipes in this book have been simplified so that they can be made at home – without a brigade of chefs to help. Most of the ingredients are widely available in supermarkets. Where something may be more difficult to find, I've tried to suggest an alternative. I also give here some notes about the ingredients I like and use most – some of which may be a little unfamiliar to you.

AROMATICS AND SEASONINGS

Maldon sea salt: I use this all the time, mainly for fish dishes, but also for preserved meats such as *confit* or ham. It has a beautiful texture and mild, salty flavour. I rarely add Maldon sea salt to a dish while it is cooking (ordinary table salt is fine for this if you need to add salt), but instead sprinkle it over the food just before serving so its rough, crunchy texture can be appreciated.

Green peppercorns: These are unripe peppercorns (the black are fully ripe). They have a subtle and interesting flavour that is especially good in a game sauce, used in small quantity. I prefer the dried peppercorns to those bottled in brine.

Herbs: I am crazy about herbs in my cooking – and they must be fresh because of their texture and flavour. I use fresh herbs in nearly every dish – one, two or three herbs, but never more or the flavours become confusing. Herbs are for me a symbol of freshness and freedom.

Bouquet garni: This bouquet or small bunch of herbs usually contains parsley, thyme and bay leaves, but you can add other aromatic ingredients depending on the recipe. For example, a bouquet garni for white meat could comprise parsley, bay leaf, tarragon, celery and onion studded with cloves; for red meat, parsley, thyme, bay leaf and tarragon; for game, thyme, bay leaf, celeriac (celery root) or celery

SALADE 'FAVORITE'
My Favourite Salad

SERVES 4

200 g/7 oz watercress
150 g/5 oz curly endive (frisé)
150 g/5 oz chicory (Belgian endive)
90 g/3 oz cooked beetroot (beets)
1 Granny Smith apple
75 g/2½ oz spring onions (scallions)
90 g/3 oz goat's cheese or Roquefort
1 tablespoon red wine vinegar
2 tablespoons walnut oil
1 tablespoon vegetable oil
freshly ground black pepper
100 g/3½ oz unsmoked streaky bacon (slices of
mild-cure bacon or salt pork)

PICK over the watercress and curly endive, discarding wilted or discoloured leaves and thick stalks. Separate the chicory leaves. Peel and dice the beetroot. Core the apple and cut into large *julienne*. Chop the spring onions. Cut the cheese into small pieces.

In a large salad bowl, combine the vinegar, oils and pepper to taste, mixing with a whisk or fork.

Remove the rind from the bacon rashers, if necessary, then cut them across into small *lardons*. Sauté them in a non-stick frying pan until crisp. Drain them on paper towels.

Add all the prepared ingredients to the salad bowl, toss with the dressing, and serve.

Illustrated opposite

Salade 'Favorite'

My Favourite Salad

PLATE 1

Coquilles St Jacques à la Grecque de Légumes

———————

Grilled Scallops with Marinated Vegetables
(recipe page 36)

PLATE 2

Gaspacho de Saumon Fumé

Gaspacho of Smoked Salmon
(recipe page 31)

PLATE 3

Canellonis de Poireaux aux Pignons de Pins

Leek and Pine Kernel Canelloni

PLATE 4

CANELLONIS DE POIREAUX AUX PIGNONS DE PINS

Leek and Pine Kernel Canelloni

SERVES 4

4 large leeks
60 g/2 oz white mushrooms
100 ml/3½ fl oz double cream (heavy cream)
1 tablespoon chopped fresh chervil
1 tablespoon chopped fresh tarragon
1 tablespoon chopped fresh parsley
a slice of white bread
3 tablespoons milk
1 egg
50 g/1¾ oz/½ cup pine kernels (pine nuts)
100 ml/3½ fl oz Nage de Légumes (page 19)
45 g/1½ oz/3 tablespoons cold unsalted butter
salt and freshly ground black pepper
¼ lemon
fresh herbs to garnish

TRIM and clean the leeks and cut them into 8 cm/3¼ inch lengths. Slit them open lengthways. Blanch the leeks in boiling salted water for 5 minutes; drain and refresh under cold running water. Reserve 16 large leaves and chop the rest. Chop the mushrooms.

Put all but 1 tablespoon of the cream in a flat pan and bring to the boil. Add the chopped leeks and mushrooms and reduce until very thick and syrupy. Add the chopped herbs and cook, stirring, for 2 minutes. Pour this mixture into a bowl and leave to cool.

Break the bread into pieces and put in a small bowl. Add the milk and mash with a fork, then mix into the leek and herb mixture with the egg.

Toast the pine kernels under the grill (broiler) until they are nicely golden all over, shaking the pan so that they brown evenly. Reserve 20 g/⅔ oz/about 3 tablespoons of the pine kernels for the garnish, and add the rest to the leek and herb mixture.

Lay 2 leek leaves side by side, slightly overlapping, on a sheet of greased foil. Top with 2 tablespoons of the leek and herb mixture and roll into a sausage shape, twisting the foil at both ends to secure it tightly. Repeat to make 8 canelloni.

Place the canelloni in a steamer and cook for 8 minutes.

Meanwhile, put the nage in a small saucepan and bring to the boil. Drop in the reserved tablespoon of cream. Remove from the heat and whisk in the butter, in small pieces. Season to taste with salt and pepper and add a squeeze of lemon juice.

To serve, place the canelloni in the centre of hot plates and spoon the sauce round. Sprinkle over some fresh herbs and the reserved pine kernels.

Illustrated opposite

TOURIN BLANC DU SUD-OUEST AU CONFIT
Onion Soup with Duck Confit

SERVES 4

200 g/7 oz onions
45 g/1½ oz duck fat, or 4 tablespoons grapeseed or other mild oil
a bunch of fresh thyme
1 leg of duck confit, weighing about 200 g/7 oz
(see recipe for Confit de Canard au Vin aux Figues, page 86)
45 g/1½ oz garlic
½ bay leaf
100 ml/3½ oz dry white wine
750 ml/1¼ pints/3 cups Fond Blanc de Volaille (page 18)
celery salt
freshly ground black pepper
1 egg
1 tablespoon chopped fresh chives

BRUNO'S NOTES

My mother used to make this soup for us after a day's work in the vineyard.

PEEL and thinly slice the onions. Heat the duck fat or oil in a saucepan and add the onions, thyme and 2 tablespoons of water. Cook over a low heat for about 10 minutes, stirring from time to time with a wooden spoon, until the onions become quite soft. Do not let them turn brown.

Meanwhile, peel the skin from the duck confit and take the meat off the bones. Cut each piece of meat into 2 or 3 pieces.

Add the sliced garlic, bay leaf and wine to the saucepan and stir for 2 minutes, then stir in the chicken stock (or water) and the duck confit. Simmer for 15 minutes.

Season to taste with celery salt and pepper, then remove the pan from the heat. With a fork, beat the egg and whisk it quickly into the hot soup.

To serve, ladle the soup into soup bowls and sprinkle over the chives.

RAVIOLES DE NAVETS ET CHAMPIGNONS
Turnip and Wild Mushroom Ravioli

SERVES 4

300 g/10 oz mixed fresh wild mushrooms
1 large, hard turnip, weighing about 350 g/12 oz
vegetable oil
salt and freshly ground black pepper
4 teaspoons mixed chopped fresh parsley and tarragon
tarragon vinegar
45 g/1½ oz/3 tablespoons unsalted butter
2 tablespoons soy sauce
fresh herbs such as chives, chervil and dill, to garnish

TRIM and clean the wild mushrooms. Set aside.
Peel the turnip and slice it widthways very finely into paper-thin leaves. Use a mandoline for this operation as it is impossible to cut thin enough slices using a knife. From each slice of turnip, cut out a 6 cm/2½ inch diameter round. You should have 48 rounds.

Preheat the oven to 180°C/350°F/gas mark 4.

Heat a film of oil in a saucepan and add 200 g/7 oz of the mushrooms. Cook gently so that the water from the mushrooms will evaporate. Season with salt and pepper, and add 3 teaspoons of mixed parsley and tarragon. Continue to cook for 3–4 minutes, stirring occasionally.

Drain the mushrooms in a colander placed over a bowl to catch the juices. On a chopping board, chop the mushrooms very finely.

Cook the turnip rounds in boiling salted water with a drop of tarragon vinegar added for about 30 seconds. Drain and put immediately into iced water to stop the cooking. Pat the turnip rounds dry with paper towels.

Lay out half of the turnip rounds on the work surface and place a spoonful of the chopped mushrooms on the centre of each. Cover with the remaining turnip rounds, placing them neatly on top and pressing the edges together to seal.

Wet 2 clean linen towels and place one on a baking sheet. Arrange the turnip ravioli in one layer on the towel and cover with the second towel (or use a large towel, folded in half).

Melt the butter in a sauté pan, add the remaining wild mushrooms and sauté over a brisk heat for 3 minutes, stirring frequently. Keep hot.

Place the ravioli in the oven and heat for 3–4 minutes. Keep checking to be sure that the towels don't start to singe!

Meanwhile, in a small pan, warm the soy sauce with the mushroom juices and the remaining mixed parsley and tarragon.

To serve, arrange the ravioli on hot plates, pour the sauce over carefully and garnish with the sautéed mushrooms and a few fresh herbs.

BRUNO'S NOTES

You can replace the wild mushrooms with a mixture of 300 g/10 oz white button mushrooms, sliced, and 45 g/1½ oz dried morels. You will need to soak the morels in warm water for 30 minutes and then clean them thoroughly under cold running water to remove all sandy grit.

If you prefer, the ravioli can be heated in a steamer rather than in the oven. Choose a plate that will fit into the steamer and arrange the ravioli on it in layers, leaving spaces around and between them so that the steam can penetrate.

COQUILLES ST JACQUES À LA GRECQUE DE LÉGUMES
Grilled Scallops with Marinated Vegetables

SERVES 4

60 g/2 oz shallots
100 ml/3½ fl oz olive oil
1 teaspoon coriander seeds
100 ml/3½ fl oz dry white wine
1 teaspoon tomato paste
2 cloves of garlic
ground cumin (optional)
150 g/5 oz/1¼ cups button onions (pearl onions)
100 g/3½ oz/1 cup cauliflower florets
60 g/2 oz button mushrooms
75 g/2½ oz tomatoes, preferably plum-type
10 large scallops (sea scallops)
salt and freshly ground black pepper
1 tablespoon finely snipped fresh coriander (cilantro)

BRUNO'S NOTES

For a dish like this you need a good quality olive oil, such as an extra virgin (first pressing) olive oil. I would choose an Italian olive oil as I find the Spanish and Greek olive oils too bitter.

PEEL the shallots and chop very finely. Heat a film of olive oil in a sauté pan, add the shallots and coriander seeds and cook on a moderate heat for about 3 minutes. Deglaze the pan with the white wine, stirring well, then stir in the tomato paste, garlic crushed with the side of a knife, and a pinch of cumin. Leave to simmer for 5 minutes.

Peel the button onions and put into the pan with 100 ml/3½ fl oz of water. Stir to mix. Cover and leave to cook gently for 8–10 minutes.

Add the cauliflower florets and continue to cook, covered, for 8 minutes, then add the mushrooms and cook for 5 minutes longer. Remove from the heat and leave to cool completely.

Skin and seed the tomatoes and cut the flesh into small dice. Set aside.

Brush each scallop on both sides with olive oil and season with salt and pepper. Heat a cast-iron grill pan until very hot, then put on the scallops and grill for 1 minute on each side.

Using a slotted spoon, arrange the vegetables on hot plates, then moisten each serving with 1 tablespoon of the juices. Cut the scallops in half lengthways and place around the vegetables. Sprinkle over the fresh coriander and diced tomatoes, add a few drops of olive oil to each plate and serve.

Illustrated on PLATE 2

OEUFS COCOTTE À LA RATATOUILLE SAFRANÉE

Eggs in Ramekins with a Saffron-Scented Ratatouille

SERVES 4

100 g/3½ oz onions
100 g/3½ oz red sweet peppers
100 g/3½ oz courgettes (zucchini)
100 g/3½ oz aubergine (eggplant)
100 g/3½ oz plum-type tomatoes
3 tablespoons olive oil
2 cloves of garlic
a bouquet garni
saffron powder
salt and freshly ground black pepper
fresh basil (optional)
4 eggs

BRUNO'S NOTES

If fresh plum-type tomatoes are not available, you can use canned tomatoes instead. Drain the juice from a 400 g/ 14 oz can of whole peeled tomatoes, then remove the seeds and chop the tomatoes.

This is a very simple, cheap and tasty first course.

PEEL the onions; trim the sweet peppers, courgettes and aubergine. Cut the prepared vegetables into 5 mm/¼ inch dice. Skin, seed and chop the tomatoes.

In a frying pan, heat 2 tablespoons olive oil and cook the onions and sweet peppers for about 6 minutes, stirring occasionally, until soft. Remove with a slotted spoon and drain on paper towels. Add the remaining oil to the pan and heat it, then cook the courgettes and aubergine for 4 minutes or until soft. Drain on paper towels.

In a deep pan, mix together all the cooked vegetables, the tomatoes, garlic crushed with the side of a knife, and the bouquet garni. Season with a good pinch of saffron, and salt and pepper to taste. Pour in a wineglass of water. Simmer for 5 minutes. Discard the bouquet garni. If liked, stir in some chopped basil.

Divide the ratatouille among 4 ramekin dishes. Break an egg into each dish over the ratatouille. Place the dishes in a shallow, heavy-based pan and add boiling water to the pan to come three-quarters up the sides of the ramekins. Simmer gently until the egg whites are set but the yolks are still a little soft, 6–8 minutes.

Grind some pepper over the eggs and serve, with toast fingers.

QUICHE SOUFFLÉE DE CHOU-FLEUR AU BLEU

Blue Cheese and Cauliflower Soufflé Quiche

SERVES 4

250 g/9 oz/2¼ cups cauliflower florets
25 g/¾ oz/2 tablespoons unsalted butter
25 g/¾ oz/2 tablespoons plain flour
250 ml/8 fl oz milk
salt and freshly ground black pepper
freshly grated nutmeg
2 egg yolks
3 egg whites
120 g/4 oz blue cheese
75 g/2½ oz spring onions (scallions)

PASTRY
125 g/4⅓ oz/¾ cup plain flour
100 g/3½ oz/7 tablespoons unsalted butter, at room temperature
1 egg yolk
salt

FIRST make the pastry. In a food processor, combine the flour, butter, egg yolk, 2 pinches of salt and 1 tablespoon of water. Process for about 10 seconds or just until a dough is formed that clings to the blades, then turn out on to the work surface. With the palms of the hands, work the dough until it is smooth. Wrap the dough and chill for at least 30 minutes.

Meanwhile, cook the cauliflower florets in boiling salted water for about 15 minutes or until tender but not mushy (test with the point of a sharp knife). Drain in a colander and leave to cool.

In a small heavy saucepan, melt the butter until foaming, then add the flour and cook for 3 minutes, stirring constantly with a whisk. Pour in the cold milk and add 2 pinches of salt, and pepper and nutmeg to taste. Continue stirring with the whisk until the sauce boils, then lower the heat and leave the sauce to simmer gently for 15 minutes. Remove from the heat, add the egg yolks and mix very well. Cover the surface of the sauce with dampened greaseproof or parchment paper to prevent a skin forming, and set aside.

On a lightly floured surface, roll out the pastry dough to a round about 28 cm/11 inches in diameter. Use to line a 20–22 cm/8–8½ inch loose-bottomed tart tin, gently easing the dough in. Cut off the excess dough around the rim, leaving a 1.5 cm/scant ¾ inch overhang. Tuck this overhang under all around the rim so that the edge of the pastry case rises above the rim of the tin. Flute the edge and prick the bottom of the pastry case with a fork. Place in the refrigerator to rest for 15 minutes.

Preheat the oven to 190°C/375°F/gas mark 5. Place a baking sheet in the oven to heat.

BRUNO'S NOTES

This delicious, inexpensive dish can also be served as a light main course, with a mixed salad.

The best blue cheeses to use are Stilton, Roquefort or Gorgonzola, but not Danish blue cheese which is too sharp and salty.

Line the pastry case with greaseproof or parchment paper and fill it with baking beans. Place the tin on the baking sheet in the oven and bake for 10 minutes, then remove the paper and beans and bake for a further 5 minutes.

Meanwhile, in a large, clean stainless steel or glass bowl, whisk the egg whites with a tiny pinch of salt until firm but not too stiff: the mixture should hold its shape on the whisk when lifted out. Add to the sauce and fold in gently. (This operation is easy if you use a pastry scraper.) Crumble the cheese over the mixture. Add the cauliflower and chopped spring onions and mix together quickly and gently.

Pour the filling into the pastry case and level the top with the scraper. Bake for about 20 minutes or until the filling is just set and golden on the top. Serve immediately.

ENDIVES EN SURPRISE
Surprise Chicory

SERVES 4

150 g/5 oz smoked salmon
juice of ¼ lemon
cayenne or freshly ground white pepper
150 ml/5 fl oz whipping cream
4 heads of chicory (Belgian endive)
150 g/5 oz cucumber
salt
a bunch of fresh chives
a bunch of fresh dill (optional)
100 ml/3½ fl oz plain yogurt
½ teaspoon green peppercorns

PUT the smoked salmon in a food processor with 4 tablespoons of water and work to obtain a smooth consistency. Add the lemon juice and cayenne or pepper to taste. Whip the cream until stiff, then mix it with the smoked salmon purée. Put aside in the refrigerator for 5 minutes or so.

Separate the leaves individually from each head of chicory. Put some of the smoked salmon mousse in each leaf, then reshape the 4 chicory heads.

Peel the cucumber. Cut it lengthways into slices 3 mm/⅛ inch thick and then into very small dice. Spread the cucumber out on a plate, sprinkle with salt and leave to drain for 5 minutes. Then rinse the cucumber under cold running water and pat dry with paper towels.

Chop the chives and dill. Put most of the chives and all the dill in a small bowl and add the cucumber, yogurt and peppercorns crushed coarsely with the side of a knife. Stir to mix.

To serve, put a head of chicory in the centre of each plate, pour some spots of the yogurt dressing around and sprinkle over the remaining chives.

CONSOMMÉ DE CAILLES ET MIQUES AUX CÈPES

Quail Consommé Garnished with Cep Dumplings

SERVES 4

CONSOMMÉ
bones from 6 quails
(see recipe for Terrine de Caille aux Abricots Secs, page 48)
1 rasher of smoked streaky bacon (1 slice of country-style bacon)
100 g/3½ oz carrots
100 g/3½ oz onions
2 stalks of celery
150 g/5 oz white part of leeks
100 g/3½ oz tomatoes, preferably plum-type
2 cloves of garlic
2 tablespoons soy sauce
fresh chervil, to garnish

CLARIFICATION
1 skinless, boneless chicken breast (chicken breast half)
2 egg whites

MIQUES
10 g/⅓ oz dried ceps
2 prunes
1 rasher of smoked streaky bacon (1 slice of country-style bacon)
a small piece of garlic
60 g/2 oz bread
30 g/1 oz/3 tablespoons flour
2 pinches of baking powder
1 tablespoon mixed chopped fresh parsley and tarragon
1 egg
2 tablespoons milk
freshly grated nutmeg
salt and freshly ground black pepper

BRUNO'S NOTES

You can use chicken bones instead of quail bones. A dash of Sauternes will improve the consommé.

The clarification isn't as complicated as it may seem, and the result is a beautifully clear soup. Just be careful when ladling the consommé into the sieve that you don't break up the 'crust'.

If you do not have any dried ceps for the *miques*, you can use 100 g/3½ oz of fresh white mushrooms. Blanch them in the boiling consommé for 5 minutes to remove excess water, then drain and pat dry with paper towels.

PUT the quail bones and the rasher of bacon in a large pan and just cover with cold water. Bring to the boil quickly, boil for 1 minute and drain. Refresh under cold running water. (This blanching will clear impurities.)

Place the bones and bacon in a deep pan or stockpot. Peel the carrots and onions and cut into chunks. Cut the celery and leeks into chunks too. Add the prepared vegetables to the stockpot with all the remaining consommé ingredients and add fresh cold water to cover. Slowly bring to the boil, skimming any scum off the surface, then partially cover the pan and leave to simmer for 1 hour.

During this time, prepare the *miques*. Soak the ceps in warm water for

30 minutes, then rinse well to remove any hidden grit, and drain. Stone the prunes and chop coarsely. Remove the rind from the bacon, if necessary, and chop coarsely. Put the ceps, prunes and bacon in a food processor and add the garlic crushed with the side of a knife, together with all the other ingredients for the *miques*. Process until you obtain a coarse mixture that will bind together. Put this *farce* in the refrigerator to firm for at least 30 minutes.

Strain the soup through a fine sieve into a clean pan and bring back to a simmer.

Flour your hands and shape the *farce* into 1 cm/½ inch diameter balls. Add the balls to the simmering soup and cook for 20 minutes. Remove the *miques* with a slotted spoon to a shallow dish. Add a ladleful or two of the soup, and set aside in a warm place.

To clarify the consommé, put the chicken breast in the food processor with 4 tablespoons of cold water and process for 30 seconds. Turn into a bowl and add the egg whites. Mix very well, and add 4 crushed ice cubes. Bring the soup to the boil, pour in the chicken mixture and quickly mix with a large spoon. Reduce the heat to medium to bring the soup down to simmering point again and leave to cook for 15 minutes. During this time, the chicken mixture will form a sort of crust on the surface of the soup, and will collect all the impurities.

Ladle the consommé into a muslin- or cheesecloth-lined sieve placed over a clean pan, leaving the chicken and egg white 'crust' behind. When you can no longer ladle the consommé, carefully pour the remainder into the sieve. Discard the 'crust'.

To serve, reheat the consommé, put the *miques* in and ladle into 4 soup plates. Sprinkle some chervil on top to garnish.

SAUMON MARINÉ SUR L'ASSIETTE
Salmon Marinated on the Plate

SERVES 4

350 g/12 oz skinned salmon fillet
4 tablespoons olive oil
4 teaspoons Maldon sea salt
freshly ground black pepper
fresh mint and basil
juice of ½ lime

BRUNO'S NOTES

This is a very simple and refreshing first course. The herbs suggested here can be replaced by fresh coriander (cilantro) and dill, as you wish, and you can serve the salmon with a green salad and toast.

Because the salmon is not cooked, it is important to use only the very freshest fish.

SLICE the salmon fillet very finely using a very sharp knife. Arrange the slices side by side, not overlapping, on the plates to cover them. Brush the olive oil on the salmon, then sprinkle over the salt, a turn of the pepper mill for each plate, some chopped mint and basil and, finally, the lime juice. Serve immediately.

TATIN DE CÉLERI AUX TRUFFES DU PÉRIGORD
Celeriac Tart Tatin with Truffles

SERVES 4

1.4 kg/3 lb celeriac (celery root)
juice of ½ lemon
200 g/7 oz duck fat
200 ml/7 fl oz dry white wine
3 cloves of garlic
100 ml/3½ fl oz Jus de Veau (page 18) or duck stock
40 g/1⅓ oz truffles, fresh or canned
salt and freshly ground black pepper
Maldon sea salt

PASTRY
125 g/4⅓ oz/¾ cup flour
100 g/3½ oz/7 tablespoons unsalted butter, at room temperature
1 egg yolk
a pinch of salt

BRUNO'S NOTES

I created this dish in autumn, 1988, at the Inn on the Park when I first started working there.

The truffles can be replaced by chopped tarragon, but this will of course make a different dish. Also, you can use a mixture of 60 g/2 oz/4 tablespoons unsalted butter and 100 ml/3½ fl oz vegetable oil instead of duck fat.

You will have celeriac trimmings; use them in the Purée d'Hiver (page 118).

PEEL the celeriac and cut it in half. Cut each half into segments about 1 cm/½ inch wide, and trim the thin side of each segment to obtain a shape like that of an apple slice. Alternatively, cut the whole peeled celeriac into slices about 1 cm/½ inch thick; lay each round slice flat and cut it into small wedges like a pie. While the celeriac is being prepared, keep it in a bowl of cold water to which the lemon juice has been added; this will prevent the celeriac going brown.

Drop the celeriac segments into a pan of boiling salted water and blanch for 3 minutes; drain well.

Heat the duck fat in a pan, add the celeriac with the white wine and roughly chopped garlic and simmer for about 20 minutes or until the celeriac is soft.

Meanwhile, put all the ingredients for the pastry into a food processor and process for 10 seconds or just until a dough is formed that clings to the blades, then turn out on to the work surface. With the palms of your hands, work the dough until smooth. Wrap and leave to rest in the refrigerator for at least 30 minutes.

Bring the veal stock to the boil in a pan and reduce until nice and syrupy. Add the finely chopped truffles and put aside in a warm place.

Preheat the oven to 220°C/425°F/gas mark 7.

Drain the celeriac segments and use them to line four 10–12 cm/4–5 inch diameter tartlet moulds, arranging the celeriac segments side by side radiating from the centre. Season to taste.

On a floured work surface, roll out the dough to 3 mm/⅛ inch thick. Cut out 4 rounds slightly bigger than the tartlet moulds. Lay a round over each mould and, with the back of a knife blade, gently ease the edge of the dough down between the celeriac and the mould. Make a small hole in the centre of each pastry lid so that the steam can escape during baking.

Set the moulds in a roasting tin containing a little water and bake in the hot oven for 10 minutes or until the pastry is golden brown and crisp.

Turn out the tarts, upside-down, on hot plates. Glaze the tops with the truffle sauce, sprinkle around some sea salt and pepper, and serve.

RILLETTES DE CRABE ET MORUE
Shredded Crab Meat and Salt Cod Bound with Curry Mayonnaise

SERVES 4

200 g/7 oz salt cod fillet
malt vinegar
200 g// oz white crab meat, preferably freshly cooked
4 spring onions (scallions)
3 tablespoons mayonnaise
mild curry powder
juice of ⅓ lemon
2 ripe avocados
fresh dill
¼ fresh coconut
4 tablespoons Vinaigrette (page 23)

BRUNO'S NOTES

You can use frozen or canned crab meat to make this dish, but freshly cooked crab is best as it will have the taste of the sea. To get 200 g/7 oz of white crab meat, you will need to cook 1 or 2 large live crabs (according to the type of crab). Bring a pan of salted water to the boil with ½ wineglass of vinegar. Plunge the crabs into the water and simmer for 10 minutes. Remove from the heat and leave in the cooking water for a further 10 minutes, then lift out the crabs and set aside to cool completely. When cold, remove all the meat from the crabs. Any brown meat can be frozen and used in another dish.

THE day before, prepare the salt cod: put the fish in a basin of cold water to soak for 3 hours, changing the water every 30 minutes. When the water is changed, brush the cod gently with a stiff vegetable brush to loosen the salt. If the salt cod is very hard and dry, it will need to be soaked for a much longer time. After soaking, it should feel soft enough to squeeze between the fingers.

Put the cod in a pan of fresh cold water, add a dash of vinegar and bring to the boil. Boil for 10 minutes, then drain. Remove the skin and any bones and trim off any hard bits. Flake the flesh. Cover and keep in the refrigerator until ready to serve.

In a large bowl, combine the cod, crab meat, chopped spring onions, mayonnaise, 1 teaspoon curry powder and the lemon juice. Mix together with a fork.

With two large spoons, make a *quenelle* of the fish mixture in the centre of each plate. Cut the avocados in half, nick out the stones and peel them. Slice each half lengthways, not cutting all the way through at the narrow end. Gently open out the slices to resemble a fan. Place an avocado 'fan' on one side of each *quenelle*.

Sprinkle dill, a little bit of curry powder and the shredded meat from the coconut over the *quenelles*. Sprinkle the avocados with the vinaigrette. Serve immediately.

ASSIETTE DE FRUITS DE MER, PETITS LÉGUMES EN GELÉE, CRÈME D'ARTICHAUTS À L'HUILE D'OLIVE

Seafood Platter with Vegetable Aspic and an Artichoke Cream

SERVES 4

450 g/1 lb fresh cockles or small hardshell clams in shell
450 g/1 lb fresh mussels in shell
100 ml/3½ fl oz dry white wine
2 large scallops (sea scallops)
4 raw langoustines or king prawns (jumbo shrimp)
1 globe artichoke
juice of 1 lemon
salt
½ teaspoon Dijon mustard
about 100 ml/3½ fl oz olive oil
mixed salad leaves
4 spring onions (scallions)
60 g/2 oz white crab meat, preferably freshly cooked
½ tablespoon chopped fresh basil
½ tablespoon chopped fresh coriander (cilantro)
freshly ground black pepper

VEGETABLE ASPICS
300 ml/10 fl oz Fumet de Poisson (page 20)
1 egg white
½ leaf of gelatine
60 g/2 oz tomato, preferably plum-type
60 g/2 oz courgette (zucchini)
60 g/2 oz bulb of fennel
60 g/2 oz red sweet pepper

FIRST prepare the aspics. In a small saucepan, bring the fish stock to the boil. In a small bowl, beat the egg white with 1 tablespoon of water and 2 coarsely crushed ice cubes. Pour the egg white mixture into the boiling fish stock, give a stir and then reduce the heat to low. Leave to cook gently until the egg comes to the surface to form a skin.

Meanwhile, soak the ½ leaf of gelatine in a little cold water to soften it.

Strain the stock through a piece of muslin or cheesecloth stretched over a bowl or a muslin- or cheesecloth-lined sieve placed over a bowl. Squeeze the leaf of gelatine, add to the stock and stir until dissolved. Set aside.

Skin and seed the tomato and cut the flesh into 5 mm/¼ inch dice. Dice the courgette, fennel and red sweet pepper the same size. Plunge the sweet pepper and fennel dice into a pan of boiling salted water. After 2 minutes, add the courgette dice and cook for another 2 minutes. Drain in a colander and refresh in iced water. Pat dry with paper towels.

Mix all the diced vegetables with the fish stock and divide among 4 baba or other ring moulds, each about 8 cm/3¼ inches in diameter. Place these aspics in the refrigerator to set.

Scrub the cockles or clams and mussels thoroughly under cold running water. Place them in a small saucepan with the white wine, cover and cook over a high heat for about 5 minutes, shaking the pan occasionally, until the shells open (discard any that remain stubbornly closed). Drain in a colander placed over a bowl, to catch the juices. Pick the cockles or clams and mussels out of their shells and put aside in another bowl.

Cut the scallops into 1 cm/½ inch cubes. Pour the juices from the cockles and mussels back into the saucepan, add the scallops and cook for 1 minute. Remove the scallops with a slotted spoon and add to the cockles and mussels.

Twist off the heads from the langoustines. Cook the tails gently in the shellfish juices in the pan for 3 minutes. Remove the langoustines with a slotted spoon. Peel them and dice the flesh. Mix with the other shellfish, then pour over the shellfish juices. Set aside in the refrigerator.

Cut the stalk from the globe artichoke with a sharp knife. Starting from the base, cut off all the leaves by turning the artichoke around until you are left just with the artichoke bottom (*fond*). Put this into a small pan of water and add a squeeze of lemon juice and ½ teaspoon of salt. Cut out a round of greaseproof or parchment paper the same diameter as the saucepan and cut a steam hole in the centre of the paper. Place the paper round on the surface of the water. Bring to the boil, then reduce the heat and simmer for 25 minutes or until the artichoke is very soft (test it with the point of a sharp knife).

Drain the artichoke, reserving the cooking liquid, and cool it under cold running water, then remove the hairy choke with a teaspoon or your thumb. Slice the artichoke thinly and place in a blender with 2 tablespoons of the cooking liquid and the mustard. Blend briefly to mix, then with the motor running, slowly pour in 3½ tablespoons of olive oil. Set this artichoke *coulis* aside in the refrigerator.

To serve, unmould a vegetable aspic on the centre of each plate. Dress the salad leaves with a little olive oil and lemon juice, then put them into the centre of the aspic rings with the chopped spring onions. Arrange all the shellfish, including the crab meat, on the plates and sprinkle over the basil and coriander, a few drops of olive oil and a squeeze of lemon juice. Season with pepper. Surround with a ring of the artichoke *coulis*.

PIZZA DE CHAMPIGNONS
Mushroom Pizza

SERVES 4

250 g/9 oz puff pastry
20 g/²⁄₃ oz/2 tablespoons shelled pistachios (optional)
30 g/1 oz/¼ cup shelled walnuts
30 g/1 oz/3 tablespoons blanched almonds
100 g/3½ oz shallots
400 g/14 oz mixed fresh wild mushrooms or open cultivated mushrooms
60 g/2 oz/4 tablespoons unsalted butter
1 clove of garlic
1 tablespoon mixed chopped fresh flat-leaf parsley and tarragon
salt and freshly ground black pepper
200 g/7 oz mozzarella cheese

BRUNO'S NOTES

This is a delicious and unusual alternative to the traditional pizza. It can also be made into 2 pizzas, to serve 2 as a light main course, in which case the cooking time should be increased a little. Serve with a chicory (Belgian endive) and bacon salad.

ON a lightly floured surface, roll out the puff pastry to 3 mm/⅛ inch thick. Place it on a floured tray and chill in the refrigerator for about 20 minutes.

Meanwhile, if you are using pistachios, blanch them in boiling water for 3 minutes, drain and rinse under cold running water. Rub them gently in a linen towel to remove the skins.

Chop the pistachios, walnuts and almonds finely with a knife or put into the food processor for 10 seconds.

Peel and slice the shallots. Trim all the mushrooms, clean them thoroughly in cold water to remove all grit, and dry them well in a salad drainer. Cut them into pieces approximately all the same size. If using cultivated mushrooms, slice them.

In a frying pan, melt the butter over high heat and cook the mushrooms for 3 minutes, stirring frequently. Remove the mushrooms with a slotted spoon and drain in a colander. Add the shallots and garlic crushed with the side of a knife to the pan and cook in the mushroom liquid until the liquid has evaporated and the shallots are caramelised. Mix with the mushrooms, nuts, herbs, and salt and pepper to taste. Leave to cool on a plate.

Preheat the oven to 230°C/450°F/gas mark 8.

Take the puff pastry out of the refrigerator and cut it into four 15 cm/6 inch diameter rounds. With a knife, mark a ring inside each round, 5 mm/¼ inch in from the edge (this outside ring will rise during baking to make a rim). Place the pastry rounds on a lightly floured baking tray, and prick the centres of the rounds with a fork (don't prick the outside ring). Top with the mushroom mixture, spreading it out evenly but leaving the outside ring uncovered.

Bake the 'pizzas' for 8 minutes, then reduce the oven temperature to 180°C/350°F/gas mark 4 and bake for a further 4 minutes. Take the pizzas out of the oven, put some slices of mozzarella on each and bake for a further 3 minutes, to melt the cheese. Serve hot.

Filo pastry can be used instead of puff, if you prefer. Cut out four 23 cm/

9 inch squares of filo for each pizza. Stack each set of 4 squares, first brushing each square with melted clarified butter or olive oil, and placing the squares on top of each other so that the points are in a different position each time. Then roughly fold over the points and sides into the centre several times to make a 1 cm/½ inch high rim on a round that is about 15 cm/6 inches in diameter. Top with the mushroom mixture and bake at 230°C/450°F/gas mark 8 for 7 minutes, then at 180°C/350°F/gas mark 4 with the cheese topping for 3 minutes.

SALADE DE M. VINICIO
Mr Vinicio's Salad

SERVES 4

1 red sweet pepper
1 yellow sweet pepper
5 tablespoons olive oil
1 very fresh bulb of fennel
250 g/9 oz ripe plum-type tomatoes
20 black olives
1 clove of garlic
1 tablespoon balsamic vinegar
salt and freshly ground black pepper
a large bunch of fresh basil
60 g/2 oz Parmesan cheese

BRUNO'S NOTES

Mr Vinicio is the restaurant manager at the Four Seasons Restaurant. He is a keen gardener and is very proud of the vegetables and herbs he grows. Being Italian, he has a special love for fennel, sweet peppers and tomatoes, so I have given this salad his name.

PREHEAT the oven to 200°C/400°F/gas mark 6.

Place the sweet peppers in a small heavy casserole or baking tin with 4 tablespoons of olive oil and 3½ tablespoons of water. Cover with foil, place in the hot oven and cook for 10 minutes.

Lift the peppers into a bowl and cover tightly (the steam trapped inside will help loosen the skin from the flesh). Leave to cool. Reserve the juices in the casserole.

Detach the large outside leaves from the fennel and put them aside for another use. Cut the heart into very fine strips and place in a large salad bowl. Slice the tomatoes and add to the fennel with the olives, the very finely chopped garlic, the vinegar and the remaining olive oil. Season to taste with salt and pepper.

Cut the peppers open, holding them over the casserole, and peel them with a small knife. Discard the core and seeds, and chop the flesh roughly. Mix with the other vegetables. Strain the juices from the casserole through a fine sieve over the vegetables.

Divide the vegetables among the plates. Chop the basil and sprinkle over the vegetables. Cut the Parmesan into fine shavings using a vegetable peeler and scatter over the top. Serve.

TERRINE DE CAILLES AUX ABRICOTS SECS
Quail Terrine Spiked with Dried Apricots

SERVES 10-12

6 oven-ready quails
celery salt
freshly ground black pepper
3½ tablespoons brandy
60 g/2 oz shallots
170 g/5½ oz/11 tablespoons unsalted butter, at room temperature
½ teaspoon fresh thyme leaves
2 cloves of garlic
100 ml/3½ fl oz Bristol Cream sherry
150 g/5 oz chicken livers
3 eggs
100 g/3½ oz/about ¾ cup dried apricot halves
250 g/9 oz unsmoked streaky bacon rashers
(slices of mild-cure bacon or salt pork)

BRUNO'S NOTES

When boning the quails, don't worry unduly about keeping them in one piece, nor about cutting through the skin. With the bones from the quails, you can make a consommé (see recipe on page 32). If, after marinating, the quails have not absorbed all the brandy, add any that remains to the liver mixture.

If you can make the terrine 2 days in advance of serving, it will taste even better.

BONE the quails, keeping the skin on. Arrange them on a tray, skin side down, and season with celery salt and pepper. Pour over the brandy. Cover and set aside to marinate in the refrigerator.

Peel and chop the shallots. In a frying pan, melt 20 g/⅔ oz/1½ tablespoons of the butter over low heat and add the shallots, thyme and the garlic crushed with the side of a knife. Sweat, covered, until the shallots are soft, without colouring. Pour in the sherry and boil, uncovered, for 3 minutes. Remove from the heat.

Trim any dark or discoloured bits from the chicken livers, then put them in a food processor with the remaining butter, melted. Process for 1 minute. Add the eggs and shallot mixture and season with celery salt and pepper. Process briefly to mix. Pass the mixture through a fine sieve into a bowl. Cover the bowl and put into the freezer for about 10 minutes to firm the mixture.

Meanwhile, put the apricots in a saucepan, cover with cold water and bring to the boil. Simmer for 5 minutes. Drain and cool under cold running water, then place the apricots on paper towels or a clean cloth to dry.

Preheat the oven to 150°C/300°F/gas mark 2.

Remove the rind from the bacon if necessary. Line a 25 × 8 cm/10 × 3½ inch terrine dish or loaf tin with the bacon, placing the rashers side by side and arranging them so that some hang well over the edge of the dish (they will be folded back over the top of the mixture, to cover it).

Start by putting a third of the liver mixture into the terrine. Cover with half of the apricots, then place 3 boned quails side by side on top. Repeat the layers, and finish with the last third of the liver mixture. Fold back the bacon rashers over the top. Cover with a doubled sheet of foil, and a lid if available.

Place the dish or tin in a deep roasting tin containing hot water. Cook in the oven for 40–45 minutes. To check if the pâté is cooked, insert a thin knife into the centre and leave it for 5 seconds; when withdrawn, it should feel hot and dry.

Remove the dish or tin from the tin of water and leave to cool at room temperature for 1 hour. Then cover closely and keep in the refrigerator for at least 12 hours before serving.

Serve in slices, with toasted country bread and Légumes au Vinaigre (page 148) or gherkins.

MOULES MARINIÈRES AU CRESSON
Steamed Mussels with Watercress Sauce

SERVES 4

1 kg/2¼ lb or more fresh mussels
Maldon sea salt
60 g/2 oz shallots
1 clove of garlic
a bunch of fresh parsley
150 ml/5 fl oz dry white wine
a bunch of watercress
100 ml/3½ fl oz double cream (heavy cream)
60 g/2 oz/4 tablespoons cold unsalted butter
¼ lemon
freshly ground black pepper

PREPARE the mussels by rubbing them with sea salt and then rinsing them under cold running water. Finally, put them in a large basin of cold water. Throw away all mussels that rise to the surface as they will be dead (mussels must always be cooked alive).

Peel the shallots and chop with the garlic and parsley. Put the mixture in a large saucepan, add the white wine and bring to the boil. Add the mussels. Cover the pan with a lid and cook for about 10 minutes or until all the mussels are open (discard any that remain closed after this time).

Meanwhile, pick the watercress leaves off the stalks.

Remove the mussels from their cooking liquor and keep them in a warm place. Strain the liquor through a very fine sieve into a clean saucepan, pressing down on the flavourings to extract all the liquid. Bring the liquor back to the boil, add the cream and boil again. Stir in the watercress leaves and boil for 4 minutes.

Turn down the heat to very low and whisk in the butter, in small pieces. Finally, add a squeeze of lemon juice.

Divide the mussels among hot soup plates and pour the sauce over. Grind some pepper over each plate and serve.

GROS RAVIOLES D'ESCARGOTS, SALADE DE COEURS DE LAITUE AUX LARDONS

Snail Ravioli with Lettuce and Bacon

SERVES 4

120 g/4 oz unsmoked streaky bacon (mild-cure bacon or salt pork)
75 g/2½ oz mushrooms
1 clove of garlic
1 tablespoon chopped fresh parsley
a slice of white bread
200 g/7 oz canned snails
30 g/1 oz/2 tablespoons unsalted butter
2 egg yolks
salt and freshly ground black pepper
250 g/9 oz Pâtes Fraîches (page 22)
½ teaspoon Dijon mustard
½ tablespoon white wine vinegar
½ tablespoon vegetable oil, plus a little extra for frying
4 'Little Gem' lettuces (or other small romaine-type lettuce)

BRUNO'S NOTES

This is a much more sophisticated way to eat snails than the traditional snails in shell with garlic and parsley butter. It will even appeal to people who are put off by the texture and aspect of snails.

REMOVE the rind from the bacon, if necessary. In a food processor, combine two-thirds of the bacon, the mushrooms, the garlic crushed with the side of a knife, the parsley and bread. Process for 2 minutes until you obtain a rough-textured *farce*.

Drain the snails and cut them into small pieces. Melt the butter in a sauté pan until foaming and add the snails and the *farce*. Cook for 10 minutes or until nearly all the juices have evaporated, stirring occasionally. Turn the mixture into a bowl. Add the egg yolks, salt and pepper, and mix very well.

Roll out the pasta dough on a lightly floured work surface with a rolling pin, or use a pasta machine, until the dough is 2 mm/scant ⅛ inch thick. With an 8 cm/3¼ inch pastry cutter, cut out 12 rounds.

Place a spoonful of the snail stuffing on each pasta round. With a wet pastry brush, slightly dampen the edges of the rounds, then fold them over to make half-moons and press the edges together to seal. Set the ravioli aside in a cool place until ready to cook.

In a large bowl, whisk together the mustard, vinegar and oil with 2 pinches of salt. Separate the lettuces into leaves, rinse in cold water and dry.

Cut the remaining bacon across into fine *lardons*. Heat a film of oil in a frying pan and sauté the bacon until crisp. Drain on paper towels.

While the bacon is being sautéed, cook the ravioli in boiling salted water for 4 minutes. Drain in a colander and rinse under hot running water. Tip the ravioli into a bowl, spoon over 1 tablespoon of the dressing and stir gently to mix. Put the lettuce into the large bowl with the remaining dressing and toss well.

Divide the ravioli among the plates. Put the dressed lettuce on one side, sprinkle over the bacon *lardons* and serve.

CAILLE RÔTIE EN SALADE DE COLESLAW

Roasted Quails on a Coleslaw Salad

SERVES 4

4 tablespoons vegetable oil
4 oven-ready quails
1 curly endive (frisé)
1 tablespoon red wine vinegar

COLESLAW
2 egg yolks
1 teaspoon Dijon mustard
salt and freshly ground black pepper
150 ml/5 fl oz vegetable oil
90 g/3 oz carrots
90 g/3 oz white cabbage
1 Granny Smith apple
4 spring onions (scallions)
1 tablespoon red wine vinegar

PREHEAT the oven to 220°C/425°F/gas mark 7.
First make the coleslaw. Put the egg yolks in a bowl with the mustard and season with salt and pepper. Gradually pour in the oil, whisking constantly, to obtain a mayonnaise. Put aside.

Peel and grate or shred the carrots. Chop the cabbage very finely. Peel and core the apple and cut it into small strips. Chop the spring onions very finely. Mix these ingredients together with the mayonnaise and the vinegar. Set aside in the refrigerator.

Heat 2 tablespoons of oil in a sauté pan and seal and brown the quails on all sides. Turn them on to their backs and season with salt and pepper. Place in the hot oven and roast for 7–10 minutes. Remove the birds from the oven, lift on to a plate and leave to rest in a warm place for 5 minutes.

Meanwhile, trim and clean the curly endive. Dress it with the vinegar, the remaining 2 tablespoons oil, and salt and pepper to taste, and mix well.

Cut off the quail legs, then cut the breasts from the carcasses. Place the legs and breasts on a baking tray and reheat in the oven for 2 minutes.

To serve, place a good spoonful of the coleslaw on the middle of each plate, arrange the curly endive around, and place the quail pieces over the coleslaw.

TERRINE DE PETIT SALÉ, PURÉE DE POIS CASSÉS
Terrine of Pork Knuckle with Split Pea Purée

SERVES 10-12

2 kg/4½ lb salted pork knuckle (uncooked ham shank)
165 g/5½ oz carrots
165 g/5½ oz onions
4 stalks of celery
165 g/5½ oz leeks
1 bay leaf
2 cloves
8 black peppercorns
a bunch of fresh thyme
5 cloves of garlic
3½ tablespoons malt vinegar
350 g/12 oz/1¾ cups dried split peas
100 ml/3½ fl oz walnut oil
4 tablespoons tarragon vinegar
salt and freshly ground black pepper

SOAK the pork knuckle in cold water for 24 hours, changing the water every 6 hours; this will remove the excess salt.

Place the drained pork in a very large pot. Peel the carrots and onions and cut into big chunks; cut the celery and leeks into chunks. Add the vegetables to the pot with the bay leaf, cloves, peppercorns, thyme, garlic crushed with the side of a knife, and the malt vinegar. Add fresh cold water to come about 5 cm/2 inches above the level of the ingredients. Bring to the boil, then leave to simmer for 4 hours.

Remove the pot from the heat and set aside to cool until warm. Then lift out the pork. Remove the skin from the pork and reserve it. Take all the meat from the bones and trim the fat away with a knife. Drain the vegetables; reserve 200 g/7 oz and discard the remainder as well as all the flavourings. Cut the reserved vegetables into small pieces.

Line a 25 × 8 cm/10 × 3½ inch terrine or loaf tin with dampened grease-proof or parchment paper, and then with most of the skin of the knuckle. Fill with the meat alternating with the chopped vegetables. Finish with pork skin. Place a small wooden board on top of the mixture and put a heavy weight on the board to press it down. Refrigerate for at least 4 hours.

Meanwhile, put the split peas in a saucepan, cover with water to come 2 cm/¾ inch above the peas and bring to the boil. Cook gently for about 40 minutes or until tender. Drain the split peas in a colander and leave to cool. When cold, purée the split peas in a blender with the walnut oil and tarragon vinegar; season to taste with salt and pepper.

To serve, slice the terrine and put one slice on each plate. Brush the slices with walnut oil and sprinkle with pepper. Add a *quenelle* of split pea purée.

BRUNO'S NOTES

This terrine can be kept in the refrigerator, wrapped tightly, for a week.

At the Inn on the Park, I spike the terrine with some cooked foie gras, which gives a nice contrast of textures and richness.

If the pork cooking liquid is not too salty, it can be used as the base for a soup.

TERRINE DU PAUVRE
Smooth Pork Pâté

BRUNO'S NOTES

I call this dish Terrine du Pauvre (Poor Man's Terrine) because it's so cheap to make.

SERVES 10-12

50 g/1¾ oz canned anchovies
400 g/14 oz pork back fat (fresh fatback)
100 g/3½ oz onions
1 clove of garlic
1 teaspoon fresh thyme leaves
½ bay leaf
400 g/14 oz pig's liver
freshly ground black pepper
freshly grated nutmeg
thin slices of pork back fat (fresh fatback), to line dish

DRAIN the anchovies, rinse them in hot water and pat dry with paper towels. Set aside. Cut the back fat into large dice. Peel and slice the onions. Put the fat and onions in a saucepan and cover with cold water. Add the peeled garlic, thyme and bay leaf. Bring to the boil, then boil for 5 minutes. Drain in a sieve.

Turn the onion mixture into a food processor and add the anchovies and liver. Process until smooth. Season with pepper and nutmeg. Pass the mixture through a very fine sieve.

Preheat the oven to 180°C/350°F/gas mark 4.

Line a 25 × 8 cm/10 × 3½ inch aluminium terrine dish or loaf tin with the slices of back fat. Spoon in the liver mixture, spreading it evenly. Place the dish or tin in a roasting tin containing a little water. Cook in the moderate oven for about 1 hour. To test if the pâté is cooked, insert a thin knife into the centre and leave it for 5 seconds; when withdrawn, it should feel hot and dry.

Remove the dish or tin from the tin of water and leave to cool completely. When cold, cover and keep in the refrigerator for 24 hours before serving.

Serve sliced, with toast and chutney.

RISSOLES DE COQUILLES ST JACQUES À LA 'CHUTNEY' DE COURGETTES

Scallops in a Crisp Potato Shell, with a Courgette Chutney

SERVES 4

20 fresh scallops (sea scallops)
4 tablespoons olive oil
2 cloves of garlic
20 g/²⁄₃ oz fresh root ginger
3 tablespoons soy sauce
salt and freshly ground black pepper
2 baking potatoes
cornflour (cornstarch)
oil for deep frying

COURGETTE CHUTNEY
150 g/5 oz onions
250 g/9 oz courgettes (zucchini)
olive oil
25 g/³⁄₄ oz/2½ tablespoons brown sugar
1 teaspoon tomato paste
1 clove of garlic
3½ tablespoons malt vinegar
1 tablespoon Worcestershire sauce

BRUNO'S NOTES

Under a crisp potato shell, a sweet, moist scallop with a sour-spicy chutney – one of the favourites at the Inn on the Park.

FIRST make the chutney: peel and finely chop the onions; cut the courgettes into very small dice. Heat a film of olive oil in a saucepan, add the onions and courgettes and cook for about 5 minutes. Stir in the sugar, tomato paste and garlic crushed with the side of a knife. Add the vinegar and Worcestershire sauce and stir to mix. Leave to cook gently for 20 minutes. When cooked, remove from the heat and set aside.

Remove the scallops from their shells, if necessary, and trim off any membrane, leaving just the white nut of meat. Cut the scallops in half if they are very large.

Mix together the olive oil, garlic crushed with the side of a knife, the peeled and chopped ginger, soy sauce, and pepper to taste in a bowl. Add the scallops to this marinade and refrigerate for at least 4 hours.

Peel the potatoes. Square off the sides, then cut into very thin slices – about 4 × 9 cm/1³⁄₄ × 3½ inches and 1 mm thick. You can cut the slices by hand using a very sharp thin-bladed knife, but a mandoline will make the job much easier. Dry the potato slices with a linen towel. Dip them into cornflour to coat on each side, then slap them with your hands to remove excess cornflour.

You will need 2 potato slices for each scallop. Place the slices on top of each other to form a cross and set the drained scallop in the centre. Fold over the ends of the potato slices to wrap the scallop completely like a parcel, and secure the parcel with wooden cocktail sticks.

Deep fry the parcels in oil heated to 180° C/350° F until golden and crisp on all sides. Drain on paper towels and season with salt.

Quickly reheat the courgette chutney. Put the scallops on hot plates with the chutney and serve immediately.

Suggested garnish: a simple green salad

Illustrated on PLATE 8

HADDOCK EN ROBE DES CHAMPS
Smoked Haddock in Jacket Potatoes
with Herb Butter

SERVES 4

4 large baking potatoes
500 g/1 lb 2 oz smoked haddock (finnan haddie)
200 ml/7 fl oz milk
100 g/3½ oz/7 tablespoons unsalted butter, at room temperature
1 tablespoon chopped fresh parsley
1 tablespoon chopped fresh basil
1 tablespoon chopped fresh tarragon
1 clove of garlic
freshly grated nutmeg
salt and freshly ground black pepper

BRUNO'S NOTES

You can replace the smoked haddock with fresh cod, if you prefer.

P REHEAT the oven to 190° C/375° F/gas mark 5.
Scrub and prick the potatoes. Bake them for 1¼–1½ hours or until tender.

Meanwhile, put the smoked haddock in a baking dish with the milk and cover with buttered greaseproof or parchment paper. Put into the oven to poach for 10 minutes. Drain the fish, reserving the milk, and flake the flesh, discarding all skin and bones. Set aside.

Mix the butter with all the herbs and the finely chopped garlic. Roll into a sausage shape, wrap and put into the refrigerator to firm.

When the potatoes are ready, cut a slice from the top of each and scoop out most of the insides with a spoon. Mash the scooped-out potato in a bowl with the milk reserved from poaching the fish, using a fork. Add nutmeg, salt and pepper to taste.

Fill the potato shells with the mashed potato and cover with the poached haddock flakes. Top each potato with a slice of herb butter. Set the potatoes in a gratin dish and heat in the oven for 10 minutes, then serve.

Suggested garnish: a large green salad

PAVÉ DE SAUMON FUMÉ À CHAUD, PURÉE DE POMMES, JUS DE VEAU

Hot Smoked Salmon with Mashed Potatoes and Veal Stock

SERVES 4

4 pieces of salmon fillet with the skin on, weighing 150 g/5 oz each
Maldon sea salt
1 kg/2¼ lb potatoes
200 ml/7 fl oz milk
100 g/3½ oz/7 tablespoons unsalted butter
freshly grated nutmeg
300 ml/10 fl oz Jus de Veau (page 18)
a small sprig of fresh rosemary
salt and freshly ground black pepper
vegetable oil

SPRINKLE the salmon pieces on both sides with 2 tablespoons of sea salt, and put aside in a cool place.

Preheat the oven to 180°C/350°F/gas mark 4.

Peel 800 g/1¾ lb of the potatoes and cut them into big chunks. Put them in a saucepan, cover with cold water and add a little salt. Bring to the boil and cook until soft – about 25 minutes depending on the quality of the potatoes.

When cooked, drain the potatoes in a colander and put them in a roasting tin, shaking the tin to spread the potatoes out evenly. Put into the oven for about 10 minutes to dry; this will give a better result with the mashed potatoes. Pass the potatoes through a mouli or potato ricer into a saucepan.

In a small pan, combine the milk, 45 g/1½ oz/3 tablespoons of the butter and nutmeg to taste. Bring to the boil, then pour over the potato purée and mix with a wooden spoon. Melt 30 g/1 oz/2 tablespoons of the remaining butter and pour over the mashed potatoes. Set aside.

Put some charcoal briquettes into a metal smoker and, if you can find them, add some vine cuttings or wood shavings from cherry, apple or plum trees. Place a grill over the charcoal and put the smoker over a high gas flame to heat until the charcoal starts to turn red and crack.

While the smoker is heating, put the veal stock into a saucepan with the rosemary and reduce to 200 ml/7 fl oz. Set aside.

Peel and finely grate the remaining potatoes, put them in a colander and rinse under cold running water. Drain and squeeze firmly in your hands to dry the potatoes as much as possible. Put them in a bowl and season with salt and pepper. Melt the remaining butter and mix it into the potatoes.

When the smoker is ready, put the salmon pieces on the grill, cover and reduce the heat underneath the smoker to low. Leave to cook for about 10 minutes or until the outside of the salmon is firm but the inside still moist.

Meanwhile, heat a film of oil in a non-stick frying pan. Place four egg poaching rings or muffin rings, each about 8 cm/3¼ inches in diameter, on

BRUNO'S NOTES

To obtain a richer mashed potato, you can add an egg yolk when reheating.

If you don't have a smoker, you can get a similar effect with a covered barbecue. Or the salmon steaks can simply be grilled, skin side down, on a barbecue.

the pan and spoon the grated potato mixture into the rings, spreading it out evenly to make galettes about 2mm/scant ⅛ inch thick. Remove the rings. Cook the galettes over a low heat until golden and crisp on each side. Put the galettes on a tray lined with paper towels and keep hot.

Reheat the mashed potato and stir well to mix in the butter. Spoon into a piping bag fitted with a large plain tube. Pipe the potato on to the centre of each hot plate to make a well, fill with the hot rosemary-infused veal stock and cover with a crispy potato galette. Remove the skin from the salmon, place it on the galettes and sprinkle round some sea salt and pepper.
Suggested garnish: a green salad

Illustrated on PLATE 9

FILETS DE TRUITE AUX CONDIMENTS
Trout Fillets Baked with Tomatoes, Ginger, Chilli and Lemon Grass

SERVES 4

skinned fillets from 4 trout
100 g/3½ oz tomatoes, preferably plum-type
60 g/2 oz shallots
1 clove of garlic
1 small green chilli pepper
1 stick of fresh lemon grass
1 teaspoon chopped fresh root ginger
saffron powder
24 capers
1 lime
salt
4 tablespoons virgin olive oil

PREHEAT the oven to 200°C/400°F/gas mark 6.
With tweezers, pick out all the bones from the fish fillets, then set the fish aside in the refrigerator.

Cut the tomatoes in half and discard the seeds, then cut the flesh into dice and put in a bowl. Peel and very finely chop the shallots and garlic. Very finely chop the chilli pepper and lemon grass. Add these to the bowl together with the ginger, a pinch of saffron and the chopped capers. Peel the lime, removing all the white pith, then cut into segments between the dividing membrane. Add the lime segments to the bowl. Mix all these ingredients well together.

Season the fish fillets with salt and place on an oiled baking tray. Top the fillets with the tomato mixture, and pour around a wineglass of water. Place in the oven and bake for about 10 minutes.

To serve, place 2 trout fillets on each hot plate and pour over a spoonful of the cooking juices and a tablespoon of olive oil.
Suggested garnish: 'Gabaldi' Provençale (page 105)

PAVÉ DE CABILLAUD, MÉLI-MÉLO D'HERBES ET POMMES NOUVELLES
Baked Cod Topped with a Herb and New Potato Salad

SERVES 4

10 new potatoes
olive oil
4 pieces of cod fillet, each about 2 cm/³⁄₄ inch thick
salt and freshly ground black pepper
a small bunch of fresh chervil
a small bunch of fresh dill
a small bunch of fresh tarragon
a small bunch of fresh parsley
a small bunch of fresh herb fennel
100 g/3½ oz fresh rocket (arugula) leaves
100 g/3½ oz celeriac (celery root)
2 shallots
1 hard-boiled egg
3 tablespoons soy sauce
1 tablespoon balsamic vinegar
3 tablespoons walnut oil

BRUNO'S NOTES

Choose thick cod fillet, cut from the centre – after cooking, it has a lovely flaky texture.

This dish does not really require a garnish. It's simple and light, based on the moist fish and the delicacy of the fresh herb salad.

PREHEAT the oven to 180°C/350°F/gas mark 4. Cook the potatoes in boiling salted water until tender.

Put a little olive oil into an ovenproof dish and place the pieces of cod fillet in it, skin side down. Season the fish with salt and pepper. Put the dish in the oven and cook for about 7 minutes or until the flesh of the cod is white but still moist. When ready, keep the fish warm until serving.

Meanwhile, prepare the herbs by taking the leaves off the stalks. Blanch the parsley in boiling water for 15 seconds; drain and refresh in iced water, then pat dry. Finely chop the rocket. Peel and slice the celeriac, then cut into fine *julienne*. Drain the potatoes and slice them. Peel and finely chop the shallots. Finely chop the hard-boiled egg. Mix all these ingredients in a bowl.

Combine the soy sauce, balsamic vinegar and walnut oil in a small saucepan and bring to a simmer over a very low heat. Pour over the salad ingredients and mix well.

Place a piece of cod fillet in the centre of each hot plate and spoon the vegetable salad over the top. Serve immediately.

LASAGNE DE CABILLAUD AUX ALGUES

Lasagne of Fresh Cod in a Seaweed Sauce

SERVES 4

200 g/7 oz Pâtes Fraîches (page 22)
20 g/²⁄₃ oz dried seaweed (nori, wakame, or konbu)
¹⁄₃ cucumber
salt and freshly ground black pepper
vegetable oil
500 g/1 lb 2 oz fresh cod fillet
30 g/1 oz shallots
3¹⁄₂ tablespoons white wine vinegar
100 ml/3¹⁄₂ fl oz dry white wine
3¹⁄₂ tablespoons double cream (heavy cream)
100 g/3¹⁄₂ oz/7 tablespoons cold unsalted butter
a bunch of fresh dill
4 tablespoons soy sauce
juice of ¹⁄₄ lemon

ROLL out the pasta dough as thinly as possible using a pasta machine or a rolling pin. Cut out 12 rounds using a 12 cm/5 inch diameter pastry cutter. (Or cut the pasta dough into 12 cm/5 inch squares.) Cook the rounds in boiling salted water for 2 minutes, then drain and rinse under cold running water. Set the pasta rounds aside in a bowl of water.

Put the seaweed in a bowl of cold water and leave to soak for 15 minutes.

Peel the cucumber, cut it in half lengthways and remove the seeds with a teaspoon. Cut the halves across into 3 mm/¹⁄₈ inch thick slices. Mix the cucumber slices in a bowl with some salt, leave to drain for 5 minutes and then rinse with cold running water. Pat dry with paper towels and set aside. Drain the seaweed. If the pieces are large, cut them into strips. Set aside.

Heat a film of vegetable oil in a non-stick frying pan. Place the cod in the pan, skin side down, cover with a lid and cook over a medium heat for 10 minutes.

Meanwhile, peel and chop the shallots. Put them in a small saucepan with the vinegar and wine, bring to the boil and reduce until you have only 1 tablespoon of liquid left. Add the cream and bring back to the boil. Remove from the heat and whisk in the butter, in small pieces.

Pass the sauce through a very fine sieve into a clean saucepan, pressing down on the shallots to extract all the liquid. Mix in the seaweed, cucumber, chopped dill, soy sauce and lemon juice.

Skin the cod, flake the meat and stir into the sauce. Keep hot.

Reheat the pasta rounds in boiling water for 1 minute, then drain on paper towels. Place a pasta round in the centre of each hot plate and spoon over a little of the fish sauce. Repeat the layers, and finish with a pasta round. Season with pepper and serve immediately.

Illustrated on PLATE 6

FRICASSÉE DE SAUMON À L'ÉTOUFFÉE DE LÉGUMES ET VINAIGRE BALSAMIQUE

Salmon Braised on a Bed of Vegetables Flavoured with Balsamic Vinegar

SERVES 4

300 g/10 oz carrots
200 g/7 oz white part of leeks
100 g/3½ oz brown cap mushrooms
a bunch of spring onions (scallions)
300 g/10 oz chicory (Belgian endive)
¼ lemon
60 g/2 oz/4 tablespoons unsalted butter
1 clove of garlic
1 cardamom pod
curry powder
a small strip of orange zest
100 ml/3½ fl oz balsamic vinegar
salt and freshly ground black pepper
vegetable oil
4 salmon steaks, each weighing about 150 g/5 oz
1 green apple
1 teaspoon each chopped fresh tarragon and chopped fresh chives
2 teaspoons chopped fresh chervil

PEEL the carrots. Using the vegetable peeler, cut the carrots lengthways into shavings. Cut the leeks into *julienne*. Thinly slice the mushrooms and spring onions. Separate the chicory leaves, then blanch them in boiling water with a squeeze of lemon juice added for 5 minutes; drain.

Melt the butter in a flameproof casserole. Add the chicory, carrots and leeks and cook on a medium heat for about 5 minutes, stirring occasionally. Add the spring onions, mushrooms, finely chopped garlic, lightly crushed cardamom pod, 2 pinches of curry powder, the strip of orange zest and, finally, the balsamic vinegar. Stir to mix, and season with salt and pepper. Continue cooking for 10 minutes or until the vegetables start to become slightly sticky and shiny.

Meanwhile, heat a film of oil in a frying pan and fry the salmon steaks for 1 minute on each side to seal. Remove from the heat and set aside.

Peel and core the apple and cut it into thin slices.

Place the salmon steaks on top of the vegetables and sprinkle over the herbs. Add 4 tablespoons of water and the apple slices. Put a lid on the casserole and cook on a very low heat for 5 minutes.

To serve, spoon the vegetables and apple on to hot plates, place the salmon steaks on top and spoon over the sauce from the vegetables.

AILE DE RAIE POCHÉE, SAUCE TARTARE

Poached Skate Wings in a Parsley and Caper Sauce

SERVES 4

75 g/2½ oz shallots
4 skate wings, weighing in total about 1.5 kg/3½ lb
100 ml/3½ fl oz dry white wine
3½ tablespoons tarragon vinegar
salt and freshly ground black pepper
100 g/3½ oz tomatoes, preferably plum-type
25 g/¾ oz (about 2 small) gherkins or cornichons
100 ml/3½ fl oz olive oil
45 g/1½ oz/3 tablespoons unsalted butter
juice of ½ lemon
25 g/¾ oz/2 tablespoons capers
a few leaves of fresh flat-leaf parsley
1 tablespoon chopped fresh chives

PEEL and slice the shallots. Place them in a large saucepan, put the skate wings on top and add the white wine, vinegar and seasoning. Pour in enough cold water so that the liquid is level with the top of the fish. Bring to the boil, then cover the pan and cook on a medium heat for 10 minutes, depending on the thickness of the fish. (To test if the fish is cooked, cut into the thick part next to the bone: the flesh should no longer be pink.)

Meanwhile, skin, seed and dice the tomatoes. Dice or slice the gherkins.

Remove the fish from the pan and put it aside in a warm place. Strain the cooking juices through a very fine sieve into a measuring jug. Pour 100 ml/ 3½ fl oz of the juices into a blender and add the olive oil, butter and lemon juice. Blend for 2 minutes.

Pour this sauce into a small pan and add the capers, roughly torn parsley, chives, diced tomatoes and gherkins. Heat briefly, whisking constantly.

To serve, place a skate wing on the middle of each hot plate and pour the sauce over.

Suggested garnish: Spaghetti de Légumes (page 110)

Illustrated on PLATE 7

CRÉPINETTE DE BARBUE AU CHOU, BEURRE DE CIDRE

Diced Brill Wrapped in Parma Ham and Cabbage, in a Cider Butter Sauce

SERVES 4

100 g/3½ oz pig's caul
malt vinegar
400 g/14 oz skinned brill fillets
1 dessert apple
2 tablespoons chopped fresh parsley
salt and freshly ground black pepper
8 leaves of Savoy cabbage
4 thin slices of Parma ham
100 g/3½ oz shallots or onion
100 ml/3½ fl oz medium cider (hard cider)
2 tablespoons double cream (heavy cream)
125 g/4½ oz/1 stick cold unsalted butter
¼ lemon
paprika

BRUNO'S NOTES

The brill can be replaced by salmon or trout.

Don't worry about any holes in the caul because it is used just to provide a little fat and to protect the *crépinettes* during cooking. If you can't find pig's caul, you can wrap the fish and cabbage balls in muslin or cheesecloth, in which case you will have to steam the *crépinettes*, allowing 8–10 minutes.

PUT the caul in a bowl of cold water and add about ½ wineglass of malt vinegar. Leave to soak for 30 minutes.

Meanwhile, cut the brill fillets into 5 mm/¼ inch dice and put in a bowl. Peel, core and dice the apple the same size. Mix with the fish. Add the parsley and season to taste with salt and pepper. Set aside in the refrigerator.

Blanch the cabbage leaves in boiling salted water for 3 minutes; drain and refresh in iced water. Pat dry with paper towels.

Drain the caul, squeeze it dry in your hands and spread it out flat on the work surface. Cut it into 4 pieces.

Shape the fish mixture into 4 balls. Wrap each ball in 2 cabbage leaves and then in a slice of Parma ham. Finally, wrap in caul. Flatten each *crépinette* slightly and put into the refrigerator while you make the sauce.

Peel and finely chop the shallots or onion. Put in a small saucepan with the cider, bring to the boil and reduce by half. Add the cream and boil again, then whisk in the butter, in small pieces. Season with a squeeze of lemon juice. Remove the sauce from the heat and keep warm.

Cook the *crépinettes* in a frying pan over a low heat for 5 minutes on each side.

Put the *crépinettes* in the centre of hot plates and pour the cider butter sauce round. Sprinkle a little paprika over the sauce and serve.
Suggested garnish: Palets à l'Ail (page 119)

Queue de Lotte et Coques à l'Effilochée d'Endives et Laitue

Monkfish Braised in a Chicory and Lettuce Cream
(recipe page 72)

PLATE 5

Lasagne de Cabillaud aux Algues

———

Lasagne of Fresh Cod in a Seaweed Sauce
(recipe page 61)

PLATE 6

Aile de Raie Pochée, Sauce Tartare

Poached Skate Wings in a Parsley and Caper Sauce
(recipe page 63)

PLATE 7

Rissoles de Coquilles St Jacques à la 'Chutney' de Courgettes

Scallops in a Crisp Potato Shell, with a Courgette Chutney
(recipe page 56)

PLATE 8

Pavé de Saumon Fumé à Chaud, Purée de Pommes, Jus de Veau

Hot Smoked Salmon with Mashed Potatoes and Veal Stock
(recipe page 58)

PLATE 9

Maquereaux Grillés, Sauce Verte

Grilled Mackerel with a Green Sauce
(recipe page 69)

PLATE 10

Filet de Carrelet à l'Anglaise, Sauce Ravigote

Fillet of Plaice Coated with Breadcrumbs
(recipe page 67)

PLATE 11

Nage de Coquilles St Jacques et Bigorneaux à l'Estragon et Poivre Vert

Scallops and Winkles in a Light Tarragon and Green Peppercorn Sauce
(recipe page 73)

PLATE 12

SOLETTE RÔTIE À L'HUILE DE CRUSTACÉS ET TOMATES CONFITES
Small Dover Sole Roasted with Shellfish Oil

SERVES 4

400 g/14 oz tomatoes, preferably plum-type
3½ tablespoons olive oil
a sprig of flat-leaf parsley
1 lime
4 Dover soles, weighing 350 g/12 oz each
100 g/3½ oz/⅔ cup flour
100 ml/3½ fl oz Huile de Crustacés (page 24)
45 g/1½ oz/¼ cup capers
1 tablespoon chopped fresh coriander (cilantro)
1 heaped teaspoon fresh thyme leaves and flowers
salt and freshly ground black pepper

PREHEAT the oven to 170°C/325°F/gas mark 3.
   Blanch the tomatoes in boiling water for 10 seconds; drain and refresh in iced water, then skin them. Cut into quarters and remove the seeds, then cut the tomatoes into strips. Place them on a baking tray and sprinkle over the olive oil. Put in the oven to dry for 2 hours.

Meanwhile, blanch the parsley in boiling water for 15 seconds, refresh and dry well. Chop the parsley and set aside.

Peel the lime, removing all the white pith, and cut out the segments, cutting down on either side of the dividing membranes. Set the lime segments aside.

About 20 minutes before serving, heat a film of olive oil in a large non-stick frying pan. Dip the soles in the flour to coat them on both sides, and tap them with your hands to get rid of excess flour. Place them in the pan, two at a time, and fry to give them a nice golden colour on each side. As they are fried, put them on a buttered baking tray.

Bake the soles in the oven for 5 minutes or until the flesh is white but still moist: test by making a small incision along the backbone using a sharp knife. Trim off the brittle bones on the sides of the fish, and put the fish on hot plates.

In a sauté pan, slightly heat the shellfish oil. Add all the other ingredients, including the dried tomatoes, parsley and lime segments, and stir to mix. Spoon over the fish and serve immediately.

Suggested garnishes: Fenouil Braisé (page 116) and Palets à l'Ail (page 119)

FILETS DE TRUITE À LA CRÈME DE KIPPERS À L'OSEILLE

Steamed Trout Fillets in a Creamed Kipper and Sorrel Sauce

SERVES 4

fillets from 4 trout
200 g/7 oz tomatoes, preferably plum-type
3 shallots
100 ml/3½ fl oz dry white wine
1 kipper
100 ml/3½ fl oz double cream (heavy cream)
juice of 1 lemon
freshly ground black pepper
100 g/3½ oz sorrel leaves
1 tablespoon chopped fresh chives

BRUNO'S NOTES

You can use salmon fillet instead of trout, but the steaming time will be longer as the fish is thicker.

WITH tweezers, pick out all the bones from the fish fillets, then set the fish aside in the refrigerator. Skin, seed and dice the tomatoes; set aside.

Peel and chop the shallots. Put them in a saucepan with the wine and bring to the boil. Boil for 2 minutes. Add the chopped kipper and cream and simmer for a further 5 minutes. Strain the sauce through a fine sieve into a small saucepan, pressing down on the kipper to extract all the liquid. Keep the sauce warm.

Take a sheet of foil and punch holes in it using the tip of a sharp knife. Lay the foil on the work surface and arrange the trout fillets on top, skin side up. Transfer the fish, on the foil, to a steamer. Sprinkle over lemon juice and pepper to taste. Cover and steam for 4 minutes.

Lift the foil out of the steamer, and remove the skin from the trout fillets. Arrange the fillets on hot plates.

Bring the sauce to the boil. Stir in the sorrel, roughly chopped, the chives, diced tomatoes and a squeeze of lemon juice. Pour the sauce over the fish, and serve.

Suggested garnish: Cannellonis d'Épinards et Artichauts (page 117) or simply boiled new potatoes

FILET DE CARRELET À L'ANGLAISE, SAUCE RAVIGOTE
Fillet of Plaice Coated with Breadcrumbs

SERVES 4

flour
1 egg
salt and freshly ground black pepper
fine dry breadcrumbs
4 skinned plaice (flounder) fillets, weighing about 600 g/1¼ lb in total
vegetable oil

SAUCE RAVIGOTE
1 egg yolk
1 tablespoon Dijon mustard
salt and freshly ground black pepper
6 tablespoons vegetable oil
6 tablespoons olive oil
1 tablespoon chopped fresh parsley
1 tablespoon chopped fresh chervil
1 tablespoon chopped fresh tarragon
juice of ½ lemon
2 tablespoons very finely chopped shallot or onion

FIRST make the sauce: in a small bowl, combine the egg yolk, mustard, 2 pinches of salt and a pinch of pepper. Mix very well with a whisk, then start to pour in the two oils very slowly, whisking constantly. Keep whisking until you get a mayonnaise. Add the herbs, lemon juice, shallot or onion and 2 tablespoons of hot water and mix well. Set aside.

Prepare in front of you 4 plates: one with flour, one with the egg beaten with 2 tablespoons of water and a little salt and pepper, one with breadcrumbs, and one empty. Pass the fish fillets through the ingredient on each of the plates in the order given, to coat both sides, finishing on the empty plate.

Heat a film of oil in a large frying pan. Put in 2 of the fish fillets and cook for 5 minutes on each side or until a nice golden brown. Lift the fillets out of the pan and drain them on paper towels to absorb the maximum of fat. Keep hot while you fry the remaining fillets.

Arrange the fish fillets on hot plates with 2 *quenelles* of sauce on each side (you can make the shape of the *quenelles* with the help of 2 tablespoons). Serve hot.

Suggested garnishes: Pommes de Terre Frites (page 106), Maldon sea salt and a green salad

Illustrated on PLATE 11

HOMARD RÔTI À L'ORANGE ET CARDAMOME
Roast Lobster with Orange and Cardamom

SERVES 4

4 live lobsters, about 700 g/1½ lb each
olive oil
100 g/3½ oz carrots
½ bulb of fennel
1 leek (white part only)
150 g/5 oz tomatoes, preferably plum-type
a bunch of fresh thyme
a strip of orange zest
3½ tablespoons brandy
100 ml/3½ fl oz dry vermouth
1 clove of garlic
3 cardamom pods or ½ teaspoon ground cardamom
4 heads of chicory (Belgian endive)
juice of ½ lemon
60 g/2 oz/4 tablespoons cold unsalted butter
salt and freshly ground black pepper

BRUNO'S NOTES

The bitterness of the chicory, the sweetness of the lobster, and the deep flavour of the cardamom and orange all combine to give this simple dish a unique character. It can also be served as a first course, for 8.

BRING a large pot of water to the boil. In the meantime, put the lobsters into the freezer to make them sleepy. When the water is boiling, plunge the lobsters into it and boil for 3 minutes. Lift out the lobsters and put them into a basin of cold water (this helps to loosen the meat from the shell).

When cool enough to handle, twist off the legs and tails from the bodies. With scissors, cut open the underside of the tail and pull out the meat. With a hammer, crack the claws and extract the meat. Coarsely break up the shells; set the meat aside.

In a large saucepan, heat 100 ml/3½ fl oz of olive oil and add the lobster shells (reserve the ends of the tails and the heads for the garnish). Stir with a wooden spatula and cook the shells for 5 minutes.

Meanwhile, peel and finely chop the carrots; finely chop the fennel and white of leek. Cut the tomatoes in half and remove the seeds, then chop the tomato flesh; set aside. Remove the lobster shells from the pan using a slotted spoon and replace with the carrots, fennel, leeks, thyme and orange zest. Cook on a low heat until the vegetables are soft, without colouring, stirring frequently.

Put the lobster shells back into the pan. Add the brandy and warm it briefly, then set alight. When the flames die down, add the vermouth, chopped tomatoes, garlic crushed with the side of a knife and the cardamom (if using cardamom pods, crush them lightly). Stir well, then simmer for 20 minutes. Pass the sauce through a very fine sieve into a clean saucepan, pressing down on the shells and flavourings in the sieve to extract all the liquid. Set aside.

In a non-stick pan, heat a film of olive oil. Add the lobster meat from the bodies and 2 tablespoons of water and cook over a moderate heat, covered, for 5 minutes. Add the meat from the lobster claws and cook for a further 5 minutes, still covered.

While the lobster is cooking, separate the chicory into leaves.

With a slotted spoon, lift the lobster meat into a soup plate and add a squeeze of lemon juice. Keep warm. Put the chicory leaves into the non-stick pan with a squeeze of lemon juice and cook for 5 minutes or until tender, stirring occasionally.

Cut the lobster meat into big chunks and arrange on hot plates with the chicory leaves. Garnish with the lobster tails and heads. Bring the sauce to the boil and whisk in the butter, in small pieces. Season to taste. Pour the sauce over the lobster meat and serve.

Suggested garnish: Polenta Grillée (page 112)

MAQUEREAUX GRILLÉS, SAUCE VERTE

Grilled Mackerel with a Green Sauce

SERVES 4

4 large bay leaves
4 mackerel, weighing about 250–350 g/9–12 oz each, cleaned and gutted
100 g/3½ oz sorrel leaves
olive oil
Maldon sea salt
freshly ground black pepper
Sauce Verte Girondine (page 20)

CUT each bay leaf into 6 strips, on a slant, using scissors. With a very sharp knife, make 3 incisions on each side of each fish and put a piece of bay leaf in each incision. Chop the sorrel and put one-quarter inside each fish. Sew up the fish or skewer closed with wooden cocktail sticks. Turn the fish in a plate of olive oil to coat on all sides.

Wrap the tails of the mackerel in foil. Put the fish under a hot grill (broiler) and cook for about 8 minutes on each side or until the flesh is white but still moist: test by making a cut along the backbone with a sharp knife.

Transfer the fish to hot plates and sprinkle some sea salt and pepper over. Serve with the sauce verte.

Suggested garnishes: Canellonis d'Épinards et Artichauts (page 117) or boiled new potatoes and a green salad

BRUNO'S NOTES

When I was a boy in the South West of France, we often ate fish that had been grilled over a fire of vine cuttings.

Illustrated on PLATE 10

QUEUE DE LOTTE ET COQUES À L'EFFILOCHÉE D'ENDIVES ET LAITUE

Monkfish Braised in a Chicory and Lettuce Cream

SERVES 4

400 g/14 oz monkfish tail
150 g/5 oz tomatoes, preferably plum-type
2 heads of chicory (Belgian endive)
1 soft-leaved lettuce
a few sprigs of fresh flat-leaf parsley
200 ml/7 fl oz dry white wine
100 ml/3½ fl oz double cream (heavy cream)
100 g/3½ oz/⅔ cup shelled freshly cooked cockles or small hardshell clams
60 g/2 oz/4 tablespoons cold unsalted butter
juice of ½ lemon
freshly ground black pepper

REMOVE any bone and membrane from the monkfish, then cut the fish into 2.5 cm/1 inch cubes.

Skin, seed and dice the tomatoes; set aside. Cut the core from the base of the chicory heads, then cut the chicory across into a fine *chiffonade*. Chop the lettuce roughly. Blanch the parsley in boiling water for 15 seconds; drain and refresh in iced water, then pat dry. Chop the parsley coarsely.

Put the monkfish cubes and white wine in a saucepan, cover with a lid and cook for 5 minutes on a low heat. Drain the fish, reserving the cooking liquor, and put aside. Pour the liquor into a clean pan and bring to the boil. Add the cream, chicory *chiffonade*, lettuce and cockles or clams. When simmering again, add the butter, cut into small pieces, the parsley, tomatoes and lemon juice. Stir well to mix. Season to taste with pepper – you should not need to add salt as the shellfish are very salty.

Put the monkfish cubes into the sauce to reheat briefly, then serve.

Suggested garnish: Pommes de Terre à l'Anis (page 107)

Illustrated on PLATE 5

NAGE DE COQUILLES ST JACQUES ET BIGORNEAUX À L'ESTRAGON ET POIVRE VERT

Scallops and Winkles in a Light Tarragon and Green Peppercorn Sauce

BRUNO'S NOTES

The success of this dish depends on the quality of the *nage*, which must be homemade.

The dish may also be served as a first course.

SERVES 4

2 litres/3½ pints/2 quarts fresh winkles (periwinkles)
10 black peppercorns
1 bay leaf
1 small green chilli pepper
Maldon sea salt
12 large scallops (sea scallops)
400 ml/14 fl oz Nage de Légumes (page 19)
12 green peppercorns
1 soft leaved lettuce
2 tablespoons double cream (heavy cream)
100 g/3½ oz/7 tablespoons cold unsalted butter
a bunch of fresh tarragon
¼ lemon

RINSE the winkles in 4 or 5 changes of water until they are very clean. Put them in a large pot, cover with 5 cm/2 inches of water and add the black peppercorns, bay leaf, chilli pepper and some sea salt. Bring to the boil and simmer for 25 minutes, then drain in a colander. Pick the winkles out of their shells one by one using a cocktail stick, and cut the little black part off the end. Set aside.

Cut the scallops in half widthways.

Bring the nage to the boil in a large flat pan. Add the green peppercorns and the chopped lettuce. Put in the scallops and winkles and turn the heat to low. Add the cream and the butter, in small pieces, and move the pan so that the liquid swirls and incorporates the butter as it melts. Taste for seasoning and add the chopped tarragon and a squeeze of lemon juice.

Put the scallops and winkles in the middle of hot soup plates and ladle the liquid over. Serve immediately.

Suggested garnish: new potatoes

Illustrated on PLATE 12

Carré d'agneau en croûte d'herbes au curcuma

Fricassée de rognons de veau au vin piqué

Filet de chevreuil dans une sauce réglisse et vin rouge

Longe de porc en cocotte à la vanille

Queue de boeuf mijotée aux pruneaux et au vinaigre

Sauté de cous d'agneau à l'orange

Râble et cuisse de lapin aux tomates douces

Volaille à l'indienne

Confit de canard au vin aux figues

Souris d'agneau aux flageolets et persil plat

Parmentier de canard

Escalope de foie de veau Mauricette

Pigeon des bois en jambon dans sa sauce à l'hydromel

Contre-filet de boeuf grillé, confit d'échalottes aux graines de moutarde

Caille rôtie, purée de pommes de terre à l'huile de noix

Poule au pot 'Henri IV', sauce verte

Jarret de veau mijoté à la sauge et à l'orange

Poulet des landes rôti à l'ail et au citron

Tétras rôties, salade tiède de navets

Pintade rôtie au céleri et ses tartines

Faisan rôti à la choucroûte fraîche, son jus à l'abricot

CHAPTER FOUR

Viandes

MEAT

I must say, the best lamb and beef I have ever tasted is British,
which must prove that Great Britain has some very superior
products. The quality of the meat in supermarkets is quite good,
the only problem being that sometimes it is not cut as it should
be. When shopping, I suggest you choose free-range poultry, and
do not hesitate to try birds such as wood pigeon or unusual cuts
of meat like neck of lamb and veal knuckle. Offal is also good
value, and can be very tasty. In preparing the recipes here, I have
tried to keep the dishes as simple as possible without too many
stocks or unnecessary garnishes on the plate – just the main
ingredients cooked in a special way, and lifted with a sauce.

CARRÉ D'AGNEAU EN CROÛTE D'HERBES AU CURCUMA

Roast Rack of Lamb with a Turmeric and Herb Crumble

SERVES 4

2 racks of lamb from best end, each with 6 bones, chined
3½ tablespoons olive oil
salt and freshly ground black pepper
100 g/3½ oz shallots
100 g/3½ oz canned Italian tomatoes (drained weight)
2 cloves of garlic
a bunch of fresh thyme
100 ml/3½ fl oz dry white wine
100 ml/3½ fl oz Jus de Veau (page 18) or 4 tablespoons soy sauce mixed
with 100 ml/3½ fl oz water
2 slices of white bread
1 tablespoon chopped fresh parsley
1 teaspoon dried herbes de Provence
½ teaspoon turmeric
2 tablespoons Meaux mustard

PREHEAT the oven to 200°C/400°F/gas mark 6.
Trim most of the fat from the racks of lamb, leaving a thin layer. Scrape off all the meat and sinews from the ends of the bones.

Heat a film of olive oil in a roasting tin on top of the stove and seal the racks of lamb on all sides. Season the lamb with salt and pepper, then place it in the hot oven and roast for 8 minutes. Turn the racks over and roast for another 8 minutes.

Meanwhile, peel and chop the shallots. Chop the tomatoes.

Remove the racks of lamb from the oven and leave to rest on a wire rack placed over a dish in a warm place for about 10 minutes.

Pour off all but 2 tablespoons of fat from the roasting tin. Add the shallots to the tin and cook over a moderate heat on top of the stove for 2 minutes. Add the tomatoes, 1 clove of garlic crushed with the side of a knife, the thyme and the white wine and stir well. Bring to the boil and simmer for 5 minutes, stirring occasionally. Stir in the veal stock and simmer for another 5 minutes. Strain through a very fine sieve or muslin or cheesecloth into a saucepan and put aside.

While the sauce is simmering, combine the bread, remaining clove of garlic, the parsley, herbes de Provence and turmeric in a food processor and process for 1 minute or until fine and evenly coloured. Heat 2 tablespoons of olive oil in a frying pan, add the bread mixture and cook over a low heat for 5 minutes, stirring with a wooden spoon, until you obtain a nice crumble that will stick together a bit. Be careful not to let it brown. Turn on to a plate.

Trim all the fat from the racks of lamb. Spread the mustard over the

BRUNO'S NOTES

We are very lucky in England to have a constantly high quality of lamb available all year round.

meaty side, then coat them in the crumble, pressing with your hands to make it stick well. Place the racks under a hot grill (broiler) until the crumble topping is nice and golden.

Meanwhile, reheat the sauce.

To serve, carefully carve the racks between the bones, place on hot plates and spoon the sauce around.

Suggested garnishes: Petites Moussakas (page 102) and some plainly cooked new vegetables

FRICASSÉE DE ROGNONS DE VEAU AU VIN PIQUÉ
Sautéed Veal Kidney in Sour Wine Sauce

SERVES 4

700 g/1½ lb veal kidney (cleaned weight)
100 g/3½ oz shallots
5 juniper berries
2 tablespoons vegetable oil
30 g/1 oz/2 tablespoons unsalted butter
1 clove of garlic
¼ bay leaf
4 tablespoons gin
100 ml/3½ fl oz sour red wine
100 ml/3½ fl oz Jus de Veau (page 18)
salt and freshly ground black pepper

BRUNO'S NOTES

If you have any wine left over after a party, keep it in an open jar in your kitchen for a week and it will become sour. Sour wine is excellent for cooking as you get all the flavours and characteristics of the wine as well as those of a good old vinegar. I particularly like to use sour wine when cooking offal.

CUT the veal kidney into 2 cm/¾ inch pieces, discarding the core. Peel the shallots and chop very finely. Heat the juniper berries in a small frying pan until they smell aromatic; set aside.

Heat the oil in a sauté pan until very hot, add the pieces of kidney and sauté for 2 minutes, stirring with a wooden spoon to cook evenly. Tip into a sieve placed over a bowl to drain. Set aside in a warm place.

In the same pan, melt the butter and add the shallots, garlic crushed with the side of a knife, the bay leaf and juniper berries. Cook for 2 minutes, then stir in the gin followed by the wine. Boil to reduce until you have only 3 tablespoons of liquid left. Add the veal stock and reduce for a further 5 minutes.

Add the juices from the kidneys. Strain the sauce through a very fine sieve into a clean pan, pressing down on the vegetables and flavourings to extract all the liquid. Add salt and pepper to taste.

Put the pieces of kidney into the sauce and reheat for 2 minutes, then serve.

Suggested garnish: Macaronis Farcis (page 109)

FILET DE CHEVREUIL DANS UNE SAUCE RÉGLISSE ET VIN ROUGE

Roast Fillet of Venison in a Liquorice-Flavoured Red Wine Sauce

SERVES 4

750 g/1 lb 10 oz piece of fillet (tenderloin) of venison
1 teaspoon juniper berries
60 g/2 oz shallots
100 g/3½ oz celeriac (celery root)
60 g/2 oz carrots
60 g/2 oz mushrooms
olive oil
a bunch of fresh thyme
1 bay leaf
2 cloves of garlic
pared zest of ½ orange
3½ tablespoons red wine vinegar
500 ml/16 fl oz full-bodied red wine
2 tablespoons dark treacle or molasses
5 tablespoons soy sauce
1½ tablespoons gin
150 g/5 oz cooked beetroot (beet)
a small piece of cold unsalted butter
freshly ground black pepper

BRUNO'S NOTES

For the sauce it is important to use a rich, strong red wine such as Madiran or a North African wine.

Venison can be replaced by lamb fillet, in which case marinate in the wine for 12 hours before cooking. (American cooks can substitute a boneless loin of lamb cut from a rack of lamb.)

TRIM the membrane and nerves from the venison and reserve. Set the meat aside in a cool place.

In a small pan, heat the juniper berries for 2 minutes (this will intensify the flavour); set aside. Peel and finely chop the shallots. Peel and dice the celeriac and carrots; dice the mushrooms.

Heat a film of olive oil in a saucepan and add the venison trimmings, the shallots, celeriac, mushrooms and carrots. Cook, stirring occasionally, until nicely golden. Add the juniper berries, thyme, bay leaf, garlic crushed with the side of a knife, and the orange zest. Deglaze the pan with the red wine vinegar, stirring well, then add the red wine and bring to the boil. Reduce by half.

Stir in the treacle or molasses, 200 ml/7 fl oz of water and the soy sauce. Leave to simmer for 1 hour or until reduced to a shiny sauce-like consistency. The dark treacle in the sauce gives it a liquorice flavour.

About 20 minutes before the sauce has finished reducing, cook the venison: heat a film of olive oil in an oval flameproof casserole and seal the meat on all sides. Reduce the heat, put the lid on the casserole and cook for about 10 minutes. Turn the venison with a spoon twice during the cooking.

Uncover the casserole, add the gin and warm it briefly, then set alight. When the flames die down, remove the venison to a rack and set aside in a warm place to rest for 5 minutes. Add the juices to the sauce.

Meanwhile, peel and dice the beetroot.

Strain the sauce through a fine sieve into a clean saucepan, pressing down on the vegetables and flavourings to extract all the liquid. Bring the sauce to the boil. Whisk in the butter, then season with pepper to taste. Add the beetroot.

Slice the venison as thick as you like, arrange on hot plates and pour the sauce over. Serve immediately.

Suggested garnish: Purée d'Hiver (page 118)

Illustrated on PLATE 14

LONGE DE PORC EN COCOTTE À LA VANILLE

Loin of Pork 'Pot-Roasted' with Vanilla

SERVES 4

1 boned loin of pork, weighing about 600 g/1¼ lb, rolled and tied
1 vanilla pod (vanilla bean)
2 cloves of garlic
salt and freshly ground black pepper
vegetable oil
6 tablespoons rice vinegar or white wine vinegar
2 tablespoons white rum
250 ml/8 fl oz canned unsweetened coconut milk

PREHEAT the oven to 180°C/350°F/gas mark 4.

With the tip of a very sharp knife, make some incisions in the skin of the pork loin. Into each cut, put a piece of vanilla pod and a thin slice of garlic dipped in salt and pepper.

Put a film of oil in a heavy flameproof casserole that is just big enough to hold the pork. Heat the oil and seal the pork all over. Turn the pork skin side up and put the lid on the casserole. Place in the oven to cook for about 20 minutes.

Pour off all the fat from the casserole. Deglaze the pot with the vinegar and rum, stirring well, then put the casserole over the heat on top of the stove and reduce for 2 minutes. Stir in the coconut milk. Put back into the oven, without the lid, and cook for a further 15 minutes or until the pork is tender and cooked through.

Lift the pork on to a rack and leave to rest in a warm place for 10 minutes, then slice and serve.

Suggested garnishes: boiled rice and Oignons au Four au Gingembre (page 116)

BRUNO'S NOTES

This is an exotic way to prepare pork. The dish does not need a sauce because the meat is so moist.

You can buy cans of coconut milk in Indian shops.

Illustrated on PLATE 16

QUEUE DE BOEUF MIJOTÉE AUX PRUNEAUX ET AU VINAIGRE

Braised Oxtail with Prunes and Vinegar

SERVES 4

1 oxtail, weighing, about 1.2 kg/2½ lb
2 onions
200 g/7 oz carrots
4 stalks of celery
300 g/10 oz leeks
vegetable oil
30 g/1 oz/2 tablespoons unsalted butter
90 g/3 oz button mushrooms
4 tablespoons red wine vinegar
100 ml/3½ fl oz Jus de Veau (page 18)
a strip of orange zest
3 cloves of garlic
1 bouquet garni
1 tablespoon Worcestershire sauce
salt and freshly ground black pepper
150 g/5 oz stoned prunes

CHOP the oxtail into chunks or have the butcher do this for you. Peel and quarter the onions. Peel and thinly slice the carrots. Cut the celery into 3 cm/1¼ inch chunks. Trim the leeks and cut into 3 cm/1¼ inch pieces.

Heat a thin film of oil in a large saucepan over high heat. Add the oxtail chunks, a few at at time, and seal and brown on all sides. Transfer to a plate.

In the same pan, melt the butter over a low heat and cook all the prepared vegetables and the mushrooms for 15 minutes or until they are nice and golden, stirring occasionally. Deglaze the pan with the vinegar, stirring well, then add the veal stock, orange zest, garlic crushed with the side of a knife, the bouquet garni, Worcestershire sauce and 500 ml/16 fl oz of water. Season to taste with salt and pepper. Bring to the boil.

Return the oxtail to the pan, and leave to simmer gently for 2½ hours. During the cooking, skim the surface of the liquid from time to time to remove all the fat.

Remove the oxtail and put to one side. Strain the cooking liquid through a fine sieve into a clean pan, pressing down on the vegetables and flavourings to extract all their liquid. Add the prunes to the cooking liquid. Bring to the boil and reduce to a shiny, sauce-like consistency.

To serve, divide the oxtail among hot soup plates and spoon the sauce over. Alternatively, you can serve the oxtail with all the cooking vegetables in the sauce.

Suggested garnish: Purée d'Hiver (page 118) or Petits Choux Farcis Grand-Mère (page 104)

Illustrated on PLATE 15

SAUTÉ DE COUS D'AGNEAU À L'ORANGE

Sauté of Neck of Lamb with Orange

SERVES 4

4 fillets of lamb, taken from the middle neck (see note)
salt and freshly ground black pepper
3 carrots
1 onion
2 large turnips
4 stalks of celery
1 orange
olive oil
½ tablespoon tomato paste
2 cloves of garlic
a branch of fresh thyme or 2 pinches of dried thyme
½ wineglass of dry white wine (optional)
4 tablespoons soy sauce
powdered saffron
chopped fresh parsley and basil (optional)

C UT the fillets across into medallions, each about 1 cm / ½ inch thick – you will probably get 6 medallions from each fillet, depending on its length. Season the medallions with salt and pepper.

Peel the carrots, onion and turnips; cut them into small dice. Dice the celery too. Pare the zest from the orange and cut it into fine *julienne*.

Heat a film of olive oil in a sauté pan. Add the lamb medallions and sauté for about 1 minute to seal and brown on both sides. Transfer them to a colander placed in a bowl to drain (the juices from the meat will be incorporated into the sauce later).

In the same pan, heat a little more oil and add all the diced vegetables. Cook over a low heat until golden, stirring occasionally. Add the tomato paste, finely chopped garlic, thyme and orange zest. Deglaze the pan with the white wine, if you are using it, and bring to the boil, stirring well. Add the juice from the orange, the soy sauce, a pinch of saffron and the juices drained from the meat. Leave to simmer for 5 minutes.

Put the lamb medallions into the sauce to reheat for about 30 seconds. Add pepper to taste, with some chopped parsley and basil if you like.

Arrange the medallions on hot plates and spoon the sauce over. Serve immediately.

Suggested garnish: fine green beans or mange-tout (snow peas)

BRUNO'S NOTES

I think the fillet from the middle neck of lamb is better than that from the best end because it is more tender and has more flavour. It is also cheaper. There is no exact equivalent American cut for lamb fillet, but American cooks can use 2 boneless loins of lamb cut from the rack of lamb, shoulder end.

If you prefer your lamb cooked medium, allow 2 minutes for the initial sautéing.

RÂBLE ET CUISSE DE LAPIN AUX TOMATES DOUCES

Roasted Saddle and Leg of Rabbit with Sun-Dried Tomatoes and Parma Ham

SERVES 4

2 saddles of rabbit (complete with bones and liver)
4 legs of rabbit
salt
1 teaspoon dried green peppercorns
100 g/3½ oz Tomates Douces Sechées au 'Soleil' (page 150)
6–8 thin slices of Parma ham

SAUCE
100 g/3½ oz carrots
100 g/3½ oz onion
60 g/2 oz celery
100 g/3½ oz white button mushrooms
four for coating
vegetable oil
1 clove of garlic
2 tablespoons light soy sauce
100 ml/3½ fl oz dry white wine
a sprig of fresh parsley
45 g/1½ oz/3 tablespoons cold unsalted butter
tarragon vinegar
freshly ground black pepper

BRUNO'S NOTES

If you are using sun-dried tomatoes in packets, they should be soaked in warm water until they soften, then drained and dried.

ASK your butcher to bone the saddles of rabbit and to keep the bones and liver.

First make the sauce: peel the carrots and onion; dice all the vegetables. Lightly flour the bones from the saddles and the rabbit legs. Heat a film of oil in a saucepan over high heat, add the bones, legs and diced vegetables and cook briskly until nicely golden brown, stirring occasionally. Add the garlic crushed with the side of a knife, the soy sauce, white wine and enough water to cover the ingredients. Bring to the boil and simmer for 35 minutes.

Meanwhile, heat a film of oil in a small frying pan and fry the rabbit liver to brown and seal it well on both sides. It should still be pink in the centre. Set aside.

Drop the parsley for the sauce into boiling water and blanch for 15 seconds, then drain and refresh in iced water. Pat dry and chop the parsley roughly. Set aside.

Preheat the oven to 200°C/400°F/gas mark 6.

Season the saddles of rabbit with a pinch of salt and sprinkle over the coarsely crushed green peppercorns. Rinse the dried tomatoes to remove any oil and pat dry with paper towels, then arrange in the fold of the saddles and place the liver on top. Roll up the saddles and wrap each one in Parma ham. Then wrap each saddle in a doubled sheet of greased foil, twisting the ends tightly to seal. Place the parcels on a baking tray and roast for 15 minutes.

Remove the saddles from the oven and leave to rest for 15 minutes.

Lift the rabbit legs out of the sauce and set aside in a warm place. Strain the sauce through a fine sieve into a clean pan, pressing down on the vegetables and flavourings to extract all the liquid. Whisk in the butter, in small pieces, and add a few drops of tarragon vinegar, the parsley, and pepper to taste.

Unwrap the foil parcels and cut each saddle across into 6 thick slices. Arrange 3 slices on each hot plate with a rabbit leg. Spoon over the sauce and serve.

Suggested garnish: young vegetables

Illustrated on PLATE 13

VOLAILLE À L'INDIENNE
Tandoori-Style Chicken

SERVES 4

4 chicken legs
125 ml/4 fl oz plain yogurt
1 tablespoon tandoori paste
salt
3 slices of white bread
2 cloves of garlic
1 teaspoon chopped fresh mint
1 teaspoon chopped fresh coriander (cilantro)
2 tablespoons olive oil
1 teaspoon curry powder

BRUNO'S NOTES
For this dish, it is important to use the leg of the chicken rather than the breast.

REMOVE the skin from the chicken legs. In a bowl, combine the yogurt, tandoori paste and 4 pinches of salt. Mix well with a spoon. Place the chicken legs in the mixture and leave to marinate in a cool place for 30 minutes.

Meanwhile, put the bread, garlic, mint, coriander, olive oil and curry powder in a food processor and process for 1 minute or until very fine. Put aside on a plate.

Preheat the oven to 180° C/350° F/gas mark 4.

Arrange the chicken legs on a rack in a baking dish and bake for 15 minutes. Remove the chicken and roll it in the bread mixture to coat all over. Put it back on the rack and bake for a further 10 minutes or until nice and golden.

Serve hot.

Suggested garnish: a raw vegetable salad or a simple, crisp 'Iceberg' lettuce salad

Filet de Chevreuil dans une Sauce Réglisse et Vin Rouge

Roast Fillet of Venison in a Liquorice-Flavoured Red Wine Sauce
(recipe page 80)

PLATE 14

Queue de Boeuf Mijotée aux Pruneaux et au Vinaigre

Braised Oxtail with Prunes and Vinegar
(recipe page 82)

PLATE 15

Faisan Rôti à la Choucroûte Fraîche, Son Jus à l'Abricot

Roast Pheasant with Braised Cabbage and an Apricot Sauce
(recipe page 98)

PLATE 18

Poule au Pot 'Henri IV', Sauce Verte

Boiled Chicken with Green Sauce
(recipe page 93)

PLATE 19

PETITS CHOUX FARCIS GRAND-MÈRE
Old-Style Stuffed Cabbage

SERVES 4

2 slices of white bread
3½ tablespoons milk
100 g/3½ oz onions
45 g/1½ oz/3 tablespoons unsalted butter or duck fat
45 g/1½ oz chicken livers
1 clove of garlic
100 g/3½ oz Parma ham or unsmoked streaky bacon (mild-cure bacon or salt pork)
1 egg
salt and freshly ground black pepper
1 tablespoon chopped fresh parsley
1 Savoy cabbage
Fond Blanc de Volaille (page 18) or water

BRUNO'S NOTES

If you like, remove 4 extra cabbage leaves and blanch them, then wrap them around the cabbage balls just before serving, for a better presentation.

SOAK the bread in the milk in a bowl; squeeze dry. Peel and chop the onions. Melt the butter or duck fat in a frying pan and sweat the onions until softened without colouring. Add the chicken livers and garlic crushed with the side of a knife and cook for 2 minutes, stirring. Turn the mixture into a food processor and add the bread, Parma ham or bacon and egg. Process for 5 seconds. Season with pepper and add the parsley. Set this *farce* aside.

Separate 8 large, outside leaves from the cabbage. Chop the rest of the cabbage, discarding the core. Blanch the cabbage leaves in boiling salted water for 3 minutes, then drain and cool in iced water. Repeat the same operation with the chopped cabbage. Dry the leaves on paper towels, and squeeze dry the chopped cabbage. Mix the chopped cabbage with the *farce*.

Cut out 4 pieces of muslin or cheesecloth, each about 20 cm/8 inches square. Lay one square of muslin or cheesecloth on the work surface and arrange 2 cabbage leaves on top, overlapping them. Spoon one-quarter of the *farce* into the centre of the cabbage and wrap the leaves around to form a ball. Enclose the ball in the cloth and tie tightly with string. Repeat to make 3 more balls.

Cook the cabbage parcels in simmering chicken stock for 15 minutes, or steam over boiling water.

Unwrap and serve hot.

Illustrated opposite

Petits Choux Farcis Grand-Mère

Old-Style Stuffed Cabbage

PLATE 21

Spaghettis de Légumes

————

Vegetable Spaghetti
(recipe page 110)

PLATE 22

Endives Braisées à l'Orange et au Poivre

Braised Chicory Flavoured with Orange and Green Peppercorns
(recipe page 113)

PLATE 23

'Gabaldi' Provençale

Gratin of Provençal Vegetables

PLATE 24

'GABALDI' PROVENÇALE
Gratin of Provençale Vegetables

SERVES 4

300 g/10 oz large courgettes (zucchini)
400 g/14 oz aubergines (eggplant)
salt and freshly ground black pepper
300 g/10 oz ripe tomatoes, preferably plum-type
3½ tablespoons olive oil
a bunch of fresh thyme
2 cloves of garlic
1 tablespoon chopped fresh basil

PREHEAT the oven to 220°C/425°F/gas mark 7.
   Cut the courgettes into 5 mm/¼ inch thick slices. Blanch them in boiling salted water for 2 minutes, then drain and refresh in iced water. Pat dry with paper towels.
   Cut the aubergines into 5 mm/¼ inch thick slices. Put them in a colander, sprinkle liberally with salt and leave to drain for 10 minutes. Rinse the slices under cold running water and pat dry with paper towels.
   Slice the tomatoes thinly.
   Arrange the courgette, aubergine and tomato slices, alternately and overlapping each other, in a gratin dish. Pour over the olive oil and crumble over the thyme. Finely chop the garlic and sprinkle on top of the sliced vegetables. Season with salt and pepper.
   Place in the hot oven and bake for 10 minutes.
   Sprinkle over the basil and serve.

Illustrated opposite

ETUVÉE DE CAROTTES AU CUMIN
Glazed Carrots Flavoured with Cumin

SERVES 4

450 g/1 lb carrots
a bunch of spring onions (scallions)
60 g/2 oz button mushrooms
60 g/2 oz/4 tablespoons unsalted butter
½ teaspoon ground cumin
½ teaspoon cumin seeds
1 clove of garlic
salt
½ tablespoon chopped fresh parsley

PEEL and thinly slice the carrots; blanch them in boiling salted water for 1 minute, then drain. Trim and chop the spring onions; thinly slice the mushrooms.

Melt the butter in a sauté pan and add the carrots, ground cumin and cumin seeds. Cover and cook on a low heat for 15 minutes, stirring 3 or 4 times.

Put in the sliced mushrooms, spring onions, garlic crushed with the side of a knife, and 2 tablespoons of water. Add salt to taste and stir well to mix. Cook for a further 5 minutes, still covered.

Just before serving, add the chopped parsley.

BRUNO'S NOTES
The parsley can be replaced by fresh coriander (cilantro) leaves.

This is an excellent garnish with beef.

CRÊPES DE POMMES DE TERRE ET MAÏS
Sweetcorn and Potato Pancakes

SERVES 4

300 g/10 oz peeled potatoes
1 egg, separated
1 tablespoon cornflour (cornstarch)
1 tablespoon double cream (heavy cream)
salt and freshly ground black pepper
100 g/3½ oz/½ cup canned sweetcorn kernels
about 60 g/2 oz/4 tablespoons unsalted butter

PREHEAT the oven to 180°C/350°F/gas mark 4.
Cut the potatoes into chunks, then cook in boiling salted water until

soft – about 25 minutes depending on the quality of the potatoes. Drain in a colander and spread out in a roasting tin. Put into the oven to dry for 10 minutes.

Pass the potatoes through a mouli or potato ricer into a bowl. Add the egg yolk, cornflour and cream and mix together using a wooden spoon. Season with salt and pepper.

Drain the canned sweetcorn on paper towels, then add to the bowl and mix with the potato. Whisk the egg white with a tiny pinch of salt until stiff, and fold gently into the sweetcorn and potato mixture.

Melt a little butter in a non-stick frying pan. Spoon in enough of the sweetcorn mixture to shape 2 pancakes, each 8 cm/3 inches in diameter and 1 cm/½ inch thick. Cook on a low heat for 4 minutes on each side. Remove the pancakes from the pan and keep them hot while you make 6 more pancakes in the same way.

Serve hot.

RISOTTO AU SAFRAN
Saffron Risotto

SERVES 4

saffron threads
3½ tablespoons dry white wine
60 g/2 oz onion
3½ tablespoons olive oil
160 g/5½ oz/¾ cup risotto rice
1 clove of garlic
500 ml/16 fl oz Fond Blanc de Volaille (page 18)
30 g/1 oz/2 tablespoons unsalted butter
15 g/½ oz/2 tablespoons Parmesan cheese
freshly ground black pepper

PUT a pinch of saffron and the wine in a small cup and leave to soak for 10 minutes.

Meanwhile, peel and chop the onion. Heat the olive oil in a large saucepan and cook the onion for 2 minutes. Add the rice and cook for 1 minute, stirring with a wooden spatula. The rice will become shiny during this time.

Add the wine and saffron mixture and the finely chopped garlic and stir to mix. Cook until the rice has absorbed the wine, then add the chicken stock, one ladleful at a time. Stir frequently and wait for the rice to absorb the stock before adding the next ladleful.

When all the stock has been added and absorbed, which will take about 15 minutes, add the butter and the freshly grated Parmesan. Cook for a further 3 minutes, stirring frequently. When cooked, the rice should have a slightly firm yet creamy consistency. Season with pepper to taste, and serve.

OIGNONS AU FOUR AU GINGEMBRE
Roasted Onions with Ginger

SERVES 4

4 large onions, preferably sweet Italian ones
45 g/1½ oz fresh root ginger
4 cloves of garlic
100 g/3½ oz/7 tablespoons unsalted butter
salt and freshly ground black pepper
100 ml/3½ fl oz white wine vinegar
1 teaspoon coriander seeds

BRUNO'S NOTES

Check the onions from time to time during roasting, and add a little more water if the liquid in the tin has evaporated.

PREHEAT the oven to 180°C/350°F/gas mark 4.
Peel the onions. Hollow out the centres with a knife to make a small hole. Peel the ginger and cut into fine *julienne*. Put a peeled clove of garlic and one-quarter of the ginger into the hole in each onion.

Place the onions in a small roasting tin. Cut the butter into 4 pieces and put one piece on each onion with some salt and pepper. Pour the vinegar into the tin and add 100 ml/3½ fl oz of water and the coriander seeds.

Put into the oven and roast for 1½ hours or until the onions are soft and caramelised, basting the onions with the juices in the tin. Serve hot.

FENOUIL BRAISÉ
Braised Fennel

SERVES 4

3½ tablespoons olive oil
4 small bulbs of fennel, or 2 very large ones cut in half
3½ tablespoons tarragon vinegar
2 cloves of garlic
1 star anise
500 ml/16 fl oz Fond Blanc de Volaille (page 18)
salt and freshly ground black pepper

HEAT the olive oil in a sauté pan, add the fennel and brown lightly on all sides. Deglaze the pan with the tarragon vinegar, stirring well, then add the garlic crushed with the side of a knife, the star anise and the chicken stock. Bring to the boil. Season very lightly with salt and pepper, then cover the pan and cook gently for 30 minutes or until the fennel is tender (test with the tip of a sharp knife).

Remove the fennel with a slotted spoon and keep hot. Boil the cooking juices until syrupy. To serve, pour the juices over the fennel.

CANELLONIS D'ÉPINARDS ET ARTICHAUTS

Spinach and Artichoke Canelloni

SERVES 4

100 g/3½ oz fresh spinach
2 globe artichokes
½ lemon
salt and freshly ground black pepper
2 slices of bread
6 tablespoons of milk
1 egg
2 cloves of garlic
250 g/9 oz Pâtes Fraîches (page 22)

REMOVE the stalks from the spinach and wash the leaves well. Blanch the leaves in boiling salted water until wilted, then drain and refresh in iced water. When cool enough to handle, squeeze the spinach in your hands to remove excess liquid. Chop the spinach roughly and set aside.

Cut the stalks off the globe artichokes with a sharp knife. Starting from the base, cut off all the leaves by turning the artichokes round, until you are left with just the bottoms or *fonds*. Put the bottoms into a pan of water. Squeeze the juice from the lemon half into the water and add the lemon half with 1 teaspoon of salt. Cut out a round of greaseproof or parchment paper to fit inside the pan, and cut a steam hole in the centre of the paper round. Place the paper on the water's surface. Bring to the boil, then simmer for 20 minutes or until the artichoke bottoms are tender (test with the tip of a sharp knife).

Drain the artichoke bottoms and remove the hairy chokes with a teaspoon or your thumb. Cut the bottoms into dice and set aside.

In a bowl, combine the bread, milk and egg, and mash them together with a fork. Add the chopped spinach, finely chopped garlic and diced artichokes and season to taste with salt and pepper.

On a lightly floured surface, roll out the pasta dough very thinly (about 1 mm). Cut out 8 squares, each about 10 × 10 cm/4 × 4 inches. Cook the pasta squares in boiling salted water for 2 minutes. Drain flat on a linen towel.

Place a piece of greased foil on the work surface. Lay one pasta square on top and put 2 tablespoons of the spinach and artichoke *farce* along the centre. Roll up to enclose the *farce*, using the foil to help lift the pasta. Wrap the canelloni in the foil, twisting the ends to seal. Repeat with the remaining pasta squares and *farce*.

Arrange the canelloni in a steamer, or stacked in a colander set in a large pan of boiling water, and cover. Steam for 5 minutes. Serve hot.

BRIOCHE PERDUE ET POIRE AU GINGEMBRE

Pan-Fried Brioche and Pear with Ginger

SERVES 4

2 large ripe pears, preferably William's (Bartlett)
120 g/4 oz/¹/₂ cup + 2 tablespoons sugar
juice of ¹/₂ lemon
¹/₂ vanilla pod (vanilla bean)
15 g/¹/₂ oz fresh root ginger
60 g/2 oz/3 tablespooons clear honey
200 ml/7 fl oz double cream (heavy cream)
dark rum
1 egg
100 ml/3¹/₂ fl oz milk
4 slices of brioche, each 2 cm/³/₄ inch thick
small piece of unsalted butter
200 ml/7 fl oz Crème Anglaise (page 25)

PEEL the pears, cut them in half lengthways and remove the cores. Put them in a saucepan with 100 g/3¹/₂ oz/¹/₂ cup of the sugar, the lemon juice and the vanilla pod. Just cover with water and put a lid on the pan. Bring to simmering point and cook gently for about 10 minutes or until the pears are just tender. (The cooking time of the pears can vary according to the quality of the fruit.) Remove from the heat and leave to cool in the syrup.

Put the remaining sugar in a small pan. Peel and chop the ginger and add to the pan with 1 tablespoon of water. Heat until the sugar has melted and turned to a nice golden caramel. Add the honey and cream and cook gently for a further 5 minutes, stirring frequently, until the caramel has dissolved in the cream. Strain through a very fine sieve into a bowl. Stir in a few drops of rum, and put aside.

In a soup plate, mix together the egg and milk. Dip both sides of the brioche slices in this mixture to soak them. Pan-fry the brioche in butter until golden brown on both sides.

To serve, place a slice of brioche on the middle of each plate with a drained pear half. Pour the crème anglaise around, and spoon the gingered caramel sauce over the pears.

Illustrated opposite

Brioche Perdue et Poire au Gingembre

Pan-Fried Brioche and Pear with Ginger

PLATE 25

Clafouti de Cerises et Pruneaux au Chocolat

Clafouti of Cherries and Prunes with Chocolate
(recipe page 131)

PLATE 26

Poire Pochée au Cassis, Glace au Lait d'Amandes

Poached Pear with Blackcurrants and Almond Ice Cream
(recipe page 137)

PLATE 27

Gelée de Framboises et Sorbet de Melon Charentais

Fresh Raspberry Jelly and Melon Sorbet
(recipe page 145)

PLATE 28

Crème Brûlée au Citron, Gelée de Citron

Lemon Crème Brûlée with a Fresh Lemon Jelly
(recipe page 132)

PLATE 29

Mille Feuille de Chocolat aux Cerises

Chocolate and Cherry Mille Feuille
(recipe page 130)

PLATE 30

Tranche de Pain d'Épices et Chocolat Blanc, Sirop de Prunes

Iced Gingerbread and White Chocolate Terrine with Prunes in Syrup
(recipe page 122)

PLATE 31

Salade de Fruits Éxotiques à l'Anis et Eau de Rose

Salad of Exotic Fruits Flavoured with Star Anise and Rosewater
(recipe page 141)

PLATE 32

TARTE À LA MOLASSE
Molasses or Dark Treacle Tart

SERVES 4

PASTRY
125 g/4⅓ oz/¾ cup flour
60 g/2 oz/4 tablespoons unsalted butter, at room temperature
1 teaspoon caster sugar (superfine sugar)
1 egg
1 egg yolk

FILLING
3 eggs
1 egg yolk
150 ml/5 fl oz double cream (heavy cream)
100 ml/3½ fl oz molasses or dark treacle
75 g/2½ oz/½ cup sultanas (golden raisins)
freshly grated nutmeg
icing sugar (confectioners' sugar)

TO make the pastry, put all the ingredients and 1½ tablespoons of cold water into a food processor and process for 10 seconds or just until a dough is formed around the blades. Turn out on to the work surface. With the palms of your hands, work the dough briefly until smooth. Wrap and leave to rest in the refrigerator for at least 30 minutes.

Roll out the dough on a lightly floured work surface until it is 3 mm/⅛ inch thick. Use to line an 18 cm/7½ inch loose-bottomed tart tin, gently easing the dough in. Cut off the excess dough around the rim, leaving a 1.5 cm/scant ¾ inch overhang. Tuck this overhang under all around the rim so that the edge of the pastry case rises above the rim of the tin. Flute the edge and prick the bottom of the pastry case with a fork. Place in the refrigerator to rest for 15 minutes.

Preheat the oven to 190°C/375°F/gas mark 5. Place a baking sheet in the oven to heat.

Line the pastry case with greaseproof or parchment paper and fill it with baking beans. Place the tin on the baking sheet in the oven and bake for 10 minutes, then remove the paper and beans and bake for a further 5 minutes.

Remove the pastry case from the oven and set it aside to cool slightly. Reduce the oven temperature to 180°C/350°F/gas mark 4.

Put the whole eggs, egg yolk, cream, molasses or treacle, sultanas and a pinch of nutmeg in a bowl and mix together. Pour the filling into the pastry case. Bake for 30 minutes or until set.

Sprinkle some sifted icing sugar over the filling. Protect the edge of the pastry case with foil, and glaze the sugar topping under the grill (broiler). Serve the tart warm.

MILLE FEUILLE DE CHOCOLAT AUX CERISES
Chocolate and Cherry Mille Feuille

SERVES 4

350 g/12 oz best-quality plain or semisweet chocolate (chocolat pâtissier)
150 g/5 oz best-quality bittersweet chocolate
20 g/²⁄₃ oz/1½ tablespoons unsalted butter
200 g/7 oz/1 cup + 3 tablespoons caster sugar (superfine sugar)
3 eggs, separated
salt
4 tablespoons whipping cream
250 g/9 oz/1 pint fresh black cherries
300 ml/10 fl oz Crème Anglaise (page 25)
1 tablespoon unsweetened cocoa powder

F IRST make the chocolate layers. Put the plain or semisweet chocolate in a heatproof bowl and set it in a pan of hot water. Stir until the chocolate is melted and smooth, then remove the bowl from the *bain-marie* of hot water.

Lay 1 or 2 perfectly clean, cut open plastic file folders (from a stationers) on a very flat tray, making sure there are no air bubbles. Spread the melted chocolate over the plastic file as thinly as possible using a rubber spatula. Leave in a cool place until almost set. Before the chocolate is completely hard, cut it with a pastry cutter or knife to make 12 rectangles, each 9 × 4 cm/3¾ × 1¾ inches. Leave to set completely on the plastic in a cool place (not the refrigerator).

Meanwhile, put the bittersweet chocolate and butter in a large heatproof bowl and set it in the *bain-marie*. Stir until melted and smooth, then stir in 1 tablespoon of the sugar until dissolved. Remove the bowl from the *bain-marie*. Incorporate the egg yolks, one by one.

Whisk the egg whites with a tiny pinch of salt until stiff, then whisk in 2 tablespoons of the remaining sugar. Whip the cream until stiff but not buttery. Fold the cream and egg whites gently but thoroughly into the chocolate mixture using a large spoon. Put into the refrigerator to set.

While the mousse is chilling, poach the cherries. Using a cherry pitter, remove the cherry stones. Put the remaining sugar in a saucepan with 500 ml/16 fl oz of water and bring to a simmer, stirring occasionally to dissolve the sugar. Add the cherries to the syrup and cook gently for 5 minutes. Remove from the heat and leave the cherries to cool in the syrup.

The chocolate leaves should now be hard. Peel them carefully from the plastic, handling them as little as possible.

Spoon the chocolate mousse into a piping bag fitted with a 1.25 cm/½ inch tube. Drain the cherries.

Pipe a little spot of mousse in the centre of each plate and place a

BRUNO'S NOTES

You can spread the melted chocolate on a sheet of parchment paper rather than the plastic file, but your chocolate leaves will not have the same shine.

For a chocolate and mint 'mille feuille', you can replace the cherries with sweetened whipped cream flavoured with mint essence (mint extract).

Any chocolate trimmings can be used in other desserts. The cherry syrup can be stored in a jar in the refrigerator and used again, to poach red fruits for example.

chocolate rectangle on top. Pipe 3 spots of mousse on the long sides of each rectangle, and place a cherry between each spot. Put another chocolate rectangle on top, and repeat the operation. Finish with a chocolate rectangle. Pour the crème anglaise around each 'mille feuille'. Sprinkle over a little cocoa powder through a sieve, and serve.

Illustrated on PLATE 30

CLAFOUTI DE CERISES ET PRUNEAUX AU CHOCOLAT
Clafouti of Cherries and Prunes with Chocolate

SERVES 4

300 g/10 oz prunes
300 g/10 oz sweet cherries (fresh or canned)
60 g/2 oz/⅔ cup ground almonds
1 tablespoon cornflour (cornstarch)
100 g/3½ oz/½ cup caster sugar (U.S. granulated sugar)
salt
20 g/⅔ oz/¼ cup unsweetened cocoa powder
2 eggs
1 egg yolk
30 g/1 oz/2 tablespoons unsalted butter
2 tablespoons double cream (heavy cream)
3 tablespoons armagnac
icing sugar (confectioners' sugar)

Illustrated on PLATE 26

BRUNO'S NOTES
You can also use the prune and cherry mixture as the filling for a *pâte sablée* tart, but bake the pastry case blind for 10 minutes first.

PUT the prunes in a bowl of hot water and leave to soak for 2 hours. Drain and remove the stones. If using canned cherries, drain them.
Preheat the oven to 180°C/350°F/gas mark 4.
In a large bowl, combine the ground almonds, cornflour, sugar, a pinch of salt, cocoa powder, whole eggs and egg yolk. Mix everything together well with a wooden spoon.
Put the butter in a small pan and heat until it has melted and turned a light brown (*noisette*). Pour it quickly into a small bowl and cool slightly, then add to the almond mixture with the cream and armagnac. Mix well.
Stir the prunes and cherries into the almond mixture. Pour into individual ramekin dishes or one large gratin dish. Set the dishes in a roasting tin and add hot water to the tin to come halfway up the sides of the ramekins. Bake for about 10 minutes.
Increase the oven heat to 190°C/375°F/gas mark 5, and bake for 5 minutes longer or until set and lightly browned.
Remove the ramekins from the *bain-marie* of hot water and cool slightly, then dredge with sifted icing sugar and serve warm with an ice cream of your choice.

CRÈME BRÛLÉE AU CITRON, GELÉE DE CITRON

Lemon Crème Brûlée with a Fresh Lemon Jelly

SERVES 4

CRÈME BRÛLÉE
3 egg yolks
150 g/5 oz/¾ cup caster sugar (U.S. granulated sugar)
2 eggs
juice of 3 lemons
juice of 1 orange
150 ml/5 fl oz double cream (heavy cream)
80 g/2⅔ oz/½ cup light brown sugar

JELLY
1 leaf of gelatine
1 lemon
50 g/1⅔ oz/¼ cup caster sugar (U.S. granulated sugar)
50 g/1⅔ oz best-quality bittersweet chocolate

BRUNO'S NOTES

For a long time I have had this crème on my menu, with a jasmine tea sorbet.

PREHEAT the oven to 180°C/350°F/gas mark 4.

First make the crèmes brûlées. In a bowl, whisk together the egg yolks and white sugar until very smooth and white. Add the whole eggs and the lemon and orange juices. Bring the cream to the boil in a small pan, then whisk it into the egg mixture.

Pour the mixture into 4 ramekin dishes. Set the dishes in a roasting tin and add enough hot water to the tin to come 1 cm/½ inch up the sides of the dishes. Place in the oven and bake for about 30 minutes or until the creams are set – touch the surface with your finger: it should not feel sticky.

In the meantime, prepare the lemon jelly. Soak the leaf of gelatine in cold water to soften it. Pare the zest from the lemon and squeeze out the juice. Combine 100 ml/3½ fl oz of water with the sugar and lemon zest in a saucepan and bring to the boil. Boil for 5 minutes, then add the lemon juice and boil for 30 seconds longer. Remove from the heat. Squeeze dry the leaf of gelatine, then add it to the lemon mixture and stir until completely dissolved. Set aside to cool, then strain to remove the lemon zest.

When the crèmes brûlées are cooked, lift them out of the *bain-marie* of hot water and set them in a tray filled with iced water. Leave to cool completely.

Put the chocolate in a small heatproof bowl and set it in the *bain-marie*. Stir until the chocolate is melted and smooth. Put the chocolate into a greaseproof or parchment paper piping cone and snip off the tip to make a tiny hole (or use a piping bag fitted with a fine writing tube). Pipe the chocolate in a triangular shape on the centre of each plate. Leave to set.

When the chocolate has set, carefully pour the lemon jelly around the outside of each chocolate triangle. Leave to set in the refrigerator.

With a thin knife blade, loosen the crèmes brûlées from the ramekins and turn them out upside-down on to a baking sheet. Cover the tops of the crèmes evenly with the brown sugar. Place under a hot grill (broiler) to melt and caramelise the sugar.

Carefully transfer the crèmes brûlées to the plates, placing them in the centre of the chocolate triangles.

Illustrated on PLATE 29

GRATIN DE PÊCHES À LA PISTACHE
Caramelised Peaches with Pistachio Cream

SERVES 4

8 medium-sized ripe but firm peaches
juice of 1 lime
2 eggs
100 g/3½ oz/½ cup caster sugar (U.S. granulated sugar)
25 g/¾ oz/2½ tablespoons flour
250 ml/8 fl oz hot milk
100 g/3½ oz shelled and peeled pistachios
30 g/1 oz/2 tablespoons unsalted butter
almond essence (almond extract)
2 egg whites
salt
4 teaspoons demerara sugar (raw brown sugar)

BRUNO'S NOTES

To remove the skins from pistachios, blanch them in boiling water for 3 minutes, then drain and rinse under cold running water. Rub them gently in a linen towel, and the skins will slip off easily.

BRING a large pot of water to the boil. Drop the peaches into the water and blanch for 2 minutes, then lift them into a bowl of iced water. Drain the peaches and slip off their skins.

Cut 2 of the peaches in half and remove the stones. Put the peaches in a blender and work to obtain a smooth *coulis*. Mix the lime juice into the *coulis*. Set aside.

Cut the remaining peaches into small wedges and use to cover the bottoms of 4 individual gratin dishes. Set aside.

In a bowl, whisk the eggs with half of the sugar until well mixed, then add the flour and hot milk. Pour into a saucepan and cook on a very low heat for 20 minutes or until quite thick, stirring from time to time with a wooden spoon. Pour this cream into the blender and add the pistachios, butter and a drop or so of almond essence to taste. Work until well combined and smooth. Transfer to a large bowl and set aside at room temperature.

In another large bowl, whisk the egg whites with a very tiny pinch of salt until stiff. Whisk in the remaining sugar. Fold the egg whites gently but thoroughly into the pistachio cream, using a large spoon.

Pour the pistachio cream over the peaches in the gratin dishes and smooth the tops. Sprinkle over the demerara sugar. Put the dishes under a preheated low grill (broiler) for 5 minutes, then turn the heat up to high, or move the dish closer to the source of heat, to caramelise the sugar.

Serve with the peach *coulis* as a sauce.

TUILES AUX ÉPICES
Spiced Almond and Coconut Biscuits

MAKES 25

100 g/3½ oz/1 cup flaked almonds (sliced almonds)
100 g/3½ oz/1 cup desiccated coconut (dried shredded coconut)
180 g/6 oz/¾ cup + 2 tablespoons caster sugar (U.S. granulated sugar)
30 g/1 oz/3 tablespoons flour
ground cinnamon
ground ginger
freshly grated nutmeg
3 egg whites (total weight 110 g/scant 4 oz)
40 g/1⅓ oz/2½ tablespoons unsalted butter, melted

IN a large bowl, combine the almonds, coconut, sugar, flour, 2 pinches of cinnamon, 4 pinches of ginger and 2 pinches of nutmeg. Add the egg whites and melted butter and mix together with a wooden spoon. Leave to rest in the refrigerator for 1 hour.

Preheat the oven to 160°C/325°F/gas mark 3.

Line several baking sheets with parchment paper. Drop teaspoonfuls of the mixture on to the paper, spacing them well apart to allow for spreading. Make them as flat as possible using a fork dipped in milk. Bake for 6–8 minutes or until a nice golden brown.

Using a slotted spatula, lift the biscuits, one by one, from the baking sheet and lay them quickly over a bottle or a rolling pin to give them the traditional roof-tile shape. Leave to cool and set on the bottle or rolling pin.

BRUNO'S NOTES

These biscuits are best baked in batches so that you can shape and cool one batch while the next one is in the oven. If you are interrupted while lifting the biscuits from the baking sheet, they may cool and become too firm to shape, but you can put them back into the oven for a few moments to soften them again.

Serve these with creamy desserts and with ice creams and sorbets. You can also shape the biscuits into cups by laying them over an orange or an upturned glass, and then fill them with a fruit salad.

CRÈME RENVERSÉE AU CARAMEL
Upside-Down Caramel Cream

SERVES 4

100 g/3½ oz Genoese or other sponge cake
a demitasse cup of very strong black coffee
100 g/3½ oz/½ cup caster sugar
½ vanilla pod (vanilla bean)
500 ml/16 fl oz milk
4 eggs

PREHEAT the oven to 190°C/375°F/gas mark 5.

Slice the sponge cake and lay the slices over the bottoms of four 9 cm/3½ inch diameter soufflé dishes, each 4.5 cm/scant 5 inches deep. Pour over the coffee and leave to soak.

BRUNO'S NOTES

When you add the boiling water to the caramel, cover your hand with an oven glove or towel because the very hot caramel is likely to spit.

Melt half of the sugar in a small saucepan and cook until it turns to a hazelnut-coloured caramel. Remove from the heat and dip the base of the pan in cold water to stop the caramel cooking. Add 1 tablespoon of boiling water to the caramel and stir to mix, then pour immediately over the sponge cake.

Split the vanilla pod open lengthways and put it in a heavy-based saucepan with the milk. Bring to the boil.

Meanwhile, mix the eggs with the remaining sugar in a bowl. Pour the boiling milk into the egg mixture, stirring well, then strain through a fine sieve into the soufflé dishes. Place the soufflé dishes in a roasting tin and pour enough hot water into the tin to come halfway up the sides of the dishes. Cook in the oven for 30 minutes or until the custard is just set.

Remove the soufflé dishes from the *bain-marie* of hot water and leave to cool completely.

To serve, turn out upside-down on to serving dishes.

SALADE DE FRUITS ÉXOTIQUES À L'ANIS ET EAU DE ROSE

Salad of Exotic Fruits Flavoured with Star Anise and Rosewater

SERVES 4

a selection of exotic fruits such as mango, papaya, passion fruit, prickly pear, guava, pineapple, kiwi fruit, grapefruit and so on
2 tablespoons rosewater

SYRUP
100 g/3½ oz/½ cup sugar
pared zest of 1 lemon
2 star anise
5 green peppercorns
a small bunch of fresh mint

T O make the syrup, put the sugar in a saucepan with 150 ml/5 fl oz of water and add the lemon zest. Bring to the boil, stirring to dissolve the sugar. Add the star anise and lightly crushed peppercorns and boil for 2 minutes. Roughly chop the mint and stir into the syrup. Remove from the heat, cover and leave to infuse and cool.

Meanwhile, peel and stone the fruits if necessary. Cut the fruits into different shapes – balls, cubes, slices and so on – and put into a bowl.

Strain the cold syrup over the fruits and put into the refrigerator to chill for at least 2 hours.

Just before serving, stir in the rosewater.

BRUNO'S NOTES

Star anise should be available in a large supermarket, and in Chinese and Indian shops. Rosewater can also be found in Indian shops.

Illustrated on PLATE 32

FIGUES CONFITES À L'ANIS, PARFAIT À LA VERVEINE

Poached Fresh Figs with Star Anise, Strega Parfait

SERVES 4

8 fresh figs
225 g/8 oz/1 cup + 2 tablespoons sugar
1 teaspoon fennel seeds
1 star anise
¼ cinnamon stick

PARFAIT
3 egg yolks
30 g/1 oz/2½ tablespoons sugar
2 tablespoons Strega liqueur or Verveine du Velay liqueur
150 ml/5 fl oz whipping cream

BRUNO'S NOTES

The components of this dessert can be prepared the day before and then dressed on the plate just before serving.

FIRST make the parfait. In a large heatproof bowl placed over a pan of simmering water, whisk the egg yolks with 2 tablespoons of hot water until five times the original volume. Remove the bowl from the hot water and set aside.

In a medium-sized saucepan, combine the sugar and 3½ tablespoons of cold water. Bring to the boil, stirring to dissolve the sugar. Boil for 2 minutes. Pour the syrup in a thin stream over the egg yolk mixture, whisking constantly, and continue whisking until cold. Add the liqueur to this *sabayon*.

In another large bowl, whip the cream until thick but not stiff. Pour the *sabayon* over the cream and fold together quickly with a large spoon.

Place four 5 cm/2 inch flan rings or muffin rings on a baking tray and fill each with the parfait mixture. Smooth the tops level. Cover and freeze for 6 hours.

While the parfait is freezing, prepare the figs. Rinse the figs very well under cold running water, then put them in a saucepan and cover with 500 ml/16 fl oz of hot water. Add the sugar, fennel seeds, star anise and cinnamon stick. Bring to a simmer, stirring occasionally to dissolve the sugar, then leave to cook gently for 30 minutes.

Remove the figs with a slotted spoon and set aside. Reduce the syrup by half. Strain the syrup into a bowl; return the star anise to the syrup and crumble in the cinnamon. Put the figs back into the syrup and leave to cool completely. When cold, put into the refrigerator to chill.

To serve, unmould the parfait rounds into soup plates and place the figs on top. Spoon over the syrup and serve immediately.

COUPE GIVRÉE MOKA
Iced Mocha Cup

SERVES 4

GRANITÉ
100 g/3½ oz/½ cup sugar
5 tablespoons instant coffee powder

CHOCOLATE MOUSSE
100 g/3½ oz best-quality bittersweet chocolate
20 g/⅔ oz/1½ tablespoons unsalted butter
3 tablespoons caster sugar (superfine sugar)
3 eggs, separated
salt

CHICORY CREAM
200 ml/7 fl oz whipping cream
chicory essence, or dark treacle or molasses
unsweetened cocoa powder

TO make the granité, put the sugar and 400 ml/14 fl oz of water in a
saucepan and bring to the boil, stirring occasionally to dissolve the
sugar. Stir in the coffee powder, then remove from the heat and allow to
cool.

Pour the cold liquid into a baking tin and put into the freezer. When 1
cm/½ inch all around the edge of the granité has set, stir this frozen mixture
into the liquid in the centre. Return to the freezer, and stir again when the
edge has set. Continue in this way, to obtain flakes of frozen granité.

While the granité is freezing, make the chocolate mousse. Put the
chocolate and butter in a heatproof bowl and set it in a pan of hot water. Stir
until the mixture is melted and smooth. Add 1 tablespoon of the sugar and
stir until it has dissolved, then remove the bowl from the *bain-marie* of hot
water. Incorporate the egg yolks, one by one.

Whisk the egg whites with a tiny pinch of salt until stiff, then whisk in
the remaining sugar. Fold the egg whites gently but thoroughly into the
chocolate mixture using a large spoon. Put into the refrigerator to set.

Whip the cream with the chicory essence or treacle or molasses until stiff
but not buttery. Keep in the refrigerator until you are ready to assemble the
dessert.

To serve, into each of 4 glass coupes, put one-quarter of the chocolate
mousse, then one-quarter of the granité, and finally one-quarter of the
chicory cream. Sprinkle the tops with a little cocoa powder through a sieve,
and serve immediately.

PÊCHES LAQUÉES AUX ÉPICES
Peaches Glazed with Spices

SERVES 4

½ teaspoon coriander seeds
½ teaspoon Szechuan pepper
⅓ stick of cinnamon
grated zest of ½ lemon
60 g/2 oz/½ cup blanched almonds
200 g/7 oz/1 cup sugar
4 large peaches
30 g/1 oz/2 tablespoons unsalted butter
5 tablespoons acacia honey
fresh mint leaves, to decorate

O N a chopping board, with the bottom of a very heavy pan, crush the spices very finely. If necessary, finish with a knife. Add the lemon zest and the coarsely chopped almonds and put aside.

Combine 1 litre/1¾ pints/1 quart of water with the sugar in a large saucepan and bring to the boil, stirring to dissolve the sugar. Put the peaches into this syrup and simmer for 2 minutes, then remove from the heat and set aside to cool. When the peaches are cool enough to handle, peel them and put them back into the syrup.

About 10 minutes before serving, melt the butter in another pan and stir in the honey and the spice mixture. Toss the drained peaches in the mixture until they are glazed (about 5 minutes.)

Spoon the peaches on to plates, sprinkle over some mint leaves, and serve with a sorbet or ice cream of your choice.

BRUNO'S NOTES

The syrup used for poaching the peaches can be kept and employed again for poaching fruit. Or add a little rosewater to taste and 1 teaspoon of egg white, and freeze in an electric ice cream machine until softly set to make a sorbet.

SALADE DE FRUITS ROUGES, GLACE AU KÜMMEL
Salad of Red Fruits with Kümmel Sorbet

SERVES 4

60 g/2 oz/5 tablespoons sugar
12 green peppercorns
a strip of orange zest
200 g/7 oz/1½ cups raspberries
150 g/5 oz/1¼ cups redcurrants
150 g/5 oz/about 1 cup strawberries
sprigs of fresh mint to decorate

BRUNO'S NOTES

If you prefer, you can make a kümmel granité rather than the sorbet. Leave out the egg white, and follow the instructions for making the granité for Coupe Givrée Moka (page 143).

SORBET
100 g/3½ oz/½ cup sugar
1 teaspoon caraway seeds
¼ egg white
1½ tablespoons kümmel

PUT the sugar in a small saucepan with 100 ml/3½ fl oz of water. Slightly crush the green peppercorns with the side of a knife and add to the pan with the orange zest. Bring to the boil, stirring to dissolve the sugar. Remove from the heat and allow to cool completely.

Combine the raspberries, redcurrants and strawberries in a bowl. Pour over the cold syrup and turn the fruits gently to mix. Leave in the refrigerator to macerate for at least 2 hours.

To make the sorbet, put the sugar and caraway seeds in a saucepan and add 200 ml/7 fl oz of water. Bring to the boil, stirring to dissolve the sugar. Strain the syrup through a fine sieve into a cold bowl. When completely cold, stir in the egg white and kümmel. Pour into an electric ice cream machine and churn for about 15 minutes or until softly set.

To serve, divide the fruits and their syrup among soup plates or dessert bowls. Add a scoop of kümmel sorbet and a sprig of fresh mint to each.

GELÉE DE FRAMBOISES ET SORBET DE MELON CHARENTAIS
Fresh Raspberry Jelly and Melon Sorbet

SERVES 4

1 leaf of gelatine
80 g/2¾ oz/6½ tablespoons sugar with pectin
500 g/1 lb 2 oz/2 pints raspberries
1 ripe melon, preferably a charentais or cavaillon with orange flesh
juice of ½ lime
¼ egg white
leaves of fresh mint, to decorate

SOAK the gelatine leaf in cold water to soften it.
Meanwhile, combine the sugar and 300 ml/10 fl oz of water in a saucepan and bring to the boil, stirring occasionally to dissolve the sugar. Remove from the heat and put the raspberries into this syrup. Squeeze the gelatine leaf and add to the raspberry mixture. Stir until the gelatine has dissolved. Divide the jelly among 4 soup plates. Place in the refrigerator to set.

Peel the melon, and remove and discard the seeds. Liquidise the flesh with the lime juice until smooth. Press the melon *coulis* through a fine sieve to remove any fibres, then pour into an electric ice cream machine and add the egg white. Churn for about 15 minutes or until softly set.

To serve, top each serving of raspberry jelly with 3 *quenelles* of melon sorbet, and garnish with mint leaves.

Illustrated on PLATE 28

Champignons à l'huile infusée

Légumes au vinaigre

'Chutney' de fruits secs

Tomates douces sechées au 'soleil'

Concombres à l'aigre doux

Fruits pochés au sirop

Kumkats aigre-doux

Vin aux figues

Vin de noix

Vin aux agrumes

Vin de framboises

Hydromel `

Cerises à la grappa

CHAPTER SEVEN

Les Conserves

PRESERVES

Preserving is a useful technique which changes the flavour and textures of certain ingredients, enabling them to be kept for a period of time. The best ingredients for preserving are those usually difficult to find or, rather, to find of good enough quality. Many of the preserves here are used quite often in my cooking.

CHAMPIGNONS À L'HUILE INFUSÉE
Mushrooms Preserved in Oil

100 g/3½ oz fresh girolles
200 g/7 oz white button mushrooms
100 ml/3½ fl oz white wine vinegar
1 teaspoon salt
3 cloves of garlic
1 bay leaf
a bunch of fresh thyme
10 black peppercorns
olive oil

TRIM and clean all the mushrooms.
   In a non-reactive saucepan, combine the vinegar, salt, the garlic slightly crushed with the side of a knife, the bay leaf, thyme, peppercorns and 200 ml/7 fl oz of water. Bring to the boil.

Add the mushrooms and blanch for 30 seconds, then drain the mushrooms and flavourings in a sieve.

Pack the mushrooms and flavourings into a clean jar and cover with olive oil. Seal and keep in a cool place.

BRUNO'S NOTES

I like these mushrooms with apéritifs or in a green salad with some croûtons. The vinegar used for blanching the mushrooms can be kept and used in salad dressings.

LÉGUMES AU VINAIGRE
Pickled Vegetables

250 g/9 oz carrots
200 g/7 oz cucumber
200 g/7 oz pickling onions
250 g/9 oz cauliflower

MARINADE
300 ml/10 fl oz white wine vinegar
1 teaspoon coriander seeds
10 black peppercorns
3 cloves of garlic
1 bay leaf
4 tablespoons clear honey
1 teaspoon mustard seed (optional)
1 teaspoon salt

PEEL the carrots and cut them across into sections 3 cm/1¼ inches long. Cut these pieces lengthways into 5 mm/¼ inch thick sticks.

BRUNO'S NOTES

Serve these pickled vegetables with pâtés, charcuterie and cold meats.

Peel the cucumber, cut it in half lengthways and remove the seeds. Then cut it into sticks the same size as the carrots.

Peel the onions. Cut the cauliflower into little florets.

In a non-reactive saucepan, combine all the ingredients for the marinade with 200 ml/7 fl oz of water. Bring to the boil and boil for 30 seconds. Add the onions and 30 seconds later add the carrots and cauliflower. Remove from the heat and leave to cool until completely cold. Then add the cucumber.

Pour the vegetables and marinade into a glass jar or bowl and cover. Leave to marinate for at least 48 hours before serving.

'CHUTNEY' DE FRUITS SECS
Dried Fruit Chutney

100 g/3½ oz dates
100 g/3½ oz prunes
100 g/3½ oz dried apricots
100 g/3½ oz dried figs
100 g/3½ oz sultanas (golden raisins)
100 g/3½ oz onions
5 cm/2 inch piece of fresh root ginger
100 g/3½ oz/7 tablespoons unsalted butter
3 cloves of garlic
5 leaves of fresh sage (optional)
1 teaspoon quatre-épices
3 tablespoons tomato paste
1 green apple
200 ml/7 fl oz malt vinegar
3 tablespoons HP Sauce
1 teaspoon salt

BRUNO'S NOTES

I love this chutney. Its sweet and sour-spicy flavour goes very well with meat pâtés. I always have a pot in my refrigerator at home.

Quatre-épices is a blend of four spices, usually cloves, ginger, pepper and nutmeg. If you cannot find it in the shops, you can substitute mixed spice.

TAKE the stones out of the dates and prunes. Put all the dried fruits in a saucepan, cover with cold water and bring to the boil. Boil for 5 minutes, then remove from the heat and set aside to soak for 1 hour. This operation will soften the fruits and extract some of the sugar.

Peel and finely chop the onions and ginger. In a large, heavy saucepan, melt the butter and cook the onions for 4–5 minutes. Add the finely chopped garlic, chopped sage leaves, ginger, *quatre-épices* and, last, the tomato paste. Stir well and leave to cook on a low heat for 5 minutes.

Meanwhile, drain the dried fruits and chop them with a knife or in the food processor for 1 minute. Peel, core and dice the apple. Add the dried fruits and apple to the onion mixture with the vinegar, HP Sauce, salt and 200 ml/7 fl oz of water. Cook very gently for 1 hour, stirring occasionally.

Leave the chutney to cool, then ladle it into jars. Cover and store in the refrigerator, where it will keep for up to 3 weeks.

TOMATES DOUCES SECHÉES AU 'SOLEIL'

'Sun-Dried' Tomatoes

2 kg/4½ lb ripe plum-type or large Italian tomatoes
salt
2 star anise
a bunch of fresh rosemary
5 cloves of garlic
1 bay leaf
virgin olive oil

PREHEAT the oven to 140°C/275°F/gas mark 1.

Cut the tomatoes in half lengthways. With a spoon, remove and discard the seeds. Sprinkle the inside of each tomato half with salt.

Put a wire rack in a baking tray and arrange the tomatoes, cut sides down, on the rack. Put them in the oven to dry for about 12 hours.

Remove the tomatoes from the oven and set aside to cool.

Drop the star anise into a small pan of boiling water and boil for 30 seconds. Drain.

In a large sterilised jar, arrange the tomatoes with the rosemary, peeled cloves of garlic, star anise and bay leaf. Pour in enough olive oil to cover. Close the jar and store in a cool, dark place for 2 weeks before using.

BRUNO'S NOTES

Of course, the original way of drying tomatoes is to put them in the sunshine, but British weather being what it is, I suggest this method instead.

It is important that the tomatoes be dried enough so that they don't give out any water if you squeeze them, but don't leave them in the oven until they become crispy.

CONCOMBRES À L'AIGRE DOUX

Pickled Cucumbers

2 cucumbers
2 tablespoons salt
200 ml/7 fl oz white wine vinegar
2 tablespoons honey
1 clove of garlic
1 teaspoon green peppercorns
20 coriander seeds
a bunch of fresh thyme
a bunch of fresh dill

PEEL the cucumbers and cut them across into 3 cm/1¼ inch sections. Trim the sections to square the sides, then cut into 1 cm/½ inch thick sticks. Don't keep any sticks that are just made up of seeds. Alternatively, cut the peeled cucumbers in half lengthways, remove the seeds and then cut crossways into 1 cm/½ inch wide half-moons.

Put the cucumber sticks in a bowl and sprinkle over 1 tablespoon of salt. Set aside for 10 minutes.

Meanwhile, combine the vinegar, honey, garlic crushed with the side of a knife, the peppercorns, coriander seeds, herbs and remaining salt in a saucepan. Bring to the boil, then remove from the heat and leave to cool completely.

Rinse the cucumber sticks under cold running water and pat dry with paper towels. Put the cucumber into a clean jar or glass bowl and pour over the cold vinegar mixture.

Cover tightly and put into the refrigerator. Leave for 2 days before using, and store in the refrigerator.

FRUITS POCHÉS AU SIROP
Poached Fruits in Syrup

fresh, ripe pears, peaches, apricots, cherries or plums
450 g/1 lb/2¼ cups sugar
1 vanilla pod (vanilla bean)
juice of ½ lemon

BRUNO'S NOTES

In winter, these fruits will be very welcome in fruit salads, as a filling for tarts, in a pavlova or in other desserts.

THE fruits used must be in perfect condition – clean and not over-ripe. Wash them in cold water, then drain in a colander, always handling with great care.

Peel and core pears, and dip them in lemon water to prevent discoloration. Blanch apricots, plums and peaches in boiling water for 1 minute, then peel, cut in half and remove the stones.

Dissolve the sugar in 1.2 litres/2 pints/5 cups of water with the vanilla pod and lemon juice. Bring slowly to the boil and boil for 1 minute. Remove from the heat and cool completely.

Pack the fruits into sterilised jars with the help of a wooden spoon. Pour in enough cold syrup to come to the top of the fruits. Tap the jar with your hands to make sure the syrup goes everywhere in the jar and that there are no air pockets. Secure the jars with spring clip and rubber band or screw-band.

Place the jars in a very large and deep pan, making sure they do not touch each other. Cover with cold water, put a lid on the pan and bring slowly to the boil. Boil gently for 15 minutes (or 30 minutes for pears). The temperature of the water should be maintained at 83°C/182°F (88°C/190°F for pears).

Lift the jars out of the water and leave them for 24 hours before testing that the seal has worked. Store in a cool, dark place.

KUMKATS AIGRE-DOUX
Pickled Kumquats

500 g/1 lb 2 oz kumquats
1 teaspoon salt
200 ml/7 fl oz white wine vinegar
1 clove
3 cardamom pods
4 tablespoons clear honey

CUT all the kumquats in half, then put them in a saucepan. Cover with cold water, add the salt and bring to the boil. Simmer for 5 minutes. Drain the fruits and allow them to cool, then chop roughly on a board.

Put the vinegar, clove, crushed cardamom pods and honey in a non-reactive saucepan and bring to the boil. Add the kumquats. Ladle the mixture into a sterilised jar, cover tightly and store in the refrigerator for 1 month before serving.

BRUNO'S NOTES

Serve this pickle with a duck or game terrine, or add a spoonful to the gravy for a roast duck.

VIN AUX FIGUES
Fig Wine

500 g/1 lb 2 oz dried figs
1 bay leaf
½ orange
1 tablespoon coriander seeds
1 stick of cinnamon
2 cardamom pods
200 ml/7 fl oz Madeira
2 litres/3½ pints/2 quarts red wine
100 ml/3½ fl oz brandy

PLACE the figs in a large saucepan and cover with cold water. Bring slowly to the boil and simmer for 5 minutes, then drain and rinse with cold water.

Return the figs to the pan and add the bay leaf, sliced orange, coriander seeds, cinnamon stick, lightly crushed cardamom pods, Madeira and red wine. Bring to the boil and simmer for 10 minutes. Remove from the heat and leave to cool completely.

Add the brandy, then pour the fig wine into jars and seal tightly. Leave for 1 month before using.

BRUNO'S NOTES

This is a wine for cooking, not drinking. It is delicious in sauces for game and red meat or in confits. To use, strain the wine; cut the figs into small cubes and add to the finished sauce.

VIN DE NOIX
Walnut Wine

20 young and very green walnuts
500 g/1 lb 2 oz/2½ cups sugar
1.5 litres/2½ pints/1½ quarts red wine
500 ml/16 fl oz brandy

BRUNO'S NOTES

You don't need to use a good quality red wine to make this.

The walnut wine can be served as an apéritif, or used in both sweet and savoury dishes, particularly for game.

In France, we have an adage that says to make a superb walnut wine, you need to pick the walnuts on the night of 29 June.

WITH a heavy knife, cut the walnuts into pieces and put them in a bowl. Add the sugar, wine and brandy and mix well. Pour into a sterilised jar, cover tightly and leave to macerate for 1 month.

Strain the wine through a sieve and then through muslin or cheesecloth. Pour it into sterilised bottles, seal with new corks and leave for 2 months before serving.

VIN AUX AGRUMES
Citrus Fruit Wine

MAKES 8 litres/14 pints/2 gallons

5 ripe oranges
4 limes
1 grapefruit
1.5 kg/3¼ lb/7½ cups sugar
5 litres/8 pints/5 quarts dry white wine, such as a Chardonnay
1.5 litres/2½ pints/1½ quarts grappa
1 vanilla pod (vanilla bean)
1 cinnamon stick
10 cardamom pods

BRUNO'S NOTES

Serve this wine with desserts, or on hot days mixed with lemonade and fresh mint like Pimm's.

Of course, you can make the wine in smaller quantities, but you'll find it goes fast.

SCRUB the fruits thoroughly and rinse well, then slice them and place in a large sterilised bowl. Mix together the sugar, wine, grappa, vanilla pod, cinnamon stick, and lightly crushed cardamom pods and pour over the fruit. Cover and leave in a cool place for 72 hours, stirring with a wooden spoon every 12 hours.

Ladle the fruit and liquid into sterilised glass preserving jars and store in a cool place for 2 months.

Strain the wine through a nylon jelly bag or a muslin- or cheesecloth-lined funnel into sterilised bottles. Boil the corks in water for 5 minutes, then use to seal the bottles. Store in a cool place.

VIN DE FRAMBOISES
Raspberry Wine

1.3 kg/2¾ lb/about 5 pints raspberries
2 litres/3½ pints/2 quarts red wine, preferably burgundy
400 g/14 oz/2 cups sugar
1 vanilla pod (vanilla bean)
300 ml/10 fl oz brandy

LIQUIDISE the raspberries to make a purée, then rub the purée through a nylon sieve to remove the seeds. You should have about 1 litre/1¾ pints/1 quart of raspberry purée.

In a large saucepan, combine the raspberry purée, wine, sugar and vanilla pod split open. Bring to the boil and boil for 30 seconds, skimming off all the scum that forms on the surface. Remove the pan from the heat, put on a lid and leave to cool completely.

Strain the liquid through muslin or cheesecloth into a bowl. Stir in the brandy. Pour this wine into sterilised bottles, seal with new corks and store in a cool place for at least 1 month before serving.

BRUNO'S NOTES

This is a wonderful dessert wine. Once opened, store it in the refrigerator.

HYDROMEL
Honey-Flavoured Wine

MAKES 2.5 litres/4 pints/2½ quarts

2 tablespoons coriander seeds
250 g/9 oz/¾ cup liquid honey
a large strip of orange zest
250 ml/8 fl oz brandy
2 litres/3½ pints/2 quarts Sauternes wine

IN a small pan, heat the coriander seeds for about 2 minutes or until you smell the strong coriander flavour.

Tip the seeds into a large bowl and add all the other ingredients. Mix well, then put into sterilised jars. Cover tightly. Set aside in a cool place to steep for 2 weeks.

Strain through a nylon jelly bag, or muslin or cheesecloth, and pour into sterilised bottles. Close each with a new cork. Store in a cool place.

BRUNO'S NOTES

I use acacia honey to make this wine. My brother, Christian, who lives in Libourne, keeps bees as a hobby – he has 30 hives – and so we are always well supplied with wonderful honey.

I like to use Hydromel in game sauces – it is a particularly good complement to a roast duck or pigeon. Add a good quantity of Hydromel when deglazing the roasting tin, then reduce with stock to make a rich sauce. Hydromel will keep quite a long time, although I've never been able to test just how long as it gets used up quickly in my kitchen.

CERISES À LA GRAPPA
Cherries in Grappa

BRUNO'S NOTES

Serve this liqueur, with the cherries, in a small liqueur glass to drink with your after-dinner coffee.

200 g/7 oz/1 cup sugar
2 strips of orange zest
500 g/1 lb 2 oz/about 2 pints fresh cherries
1 litre/1¾ pints/1 quart grappa

PUT the sugar and orange zest in a saucepan with 200 ml/7 fl oz of water. Bring to the boil, stirring to dissolve the sugar, then remove from the heat and leave to cool.

Meanwhile, wash the cherries well and dry them completely with paper towels. With scissors, trim the stalks to half their length.

Put the cherries into sterilised jars. Stir the grappa into the syrup, then pour it over the cherries to cover them. Close the jars tightly and store in a cool, dark place for at least 1 month before serving.

INDEX

ACKNOWLEDGEMENTS

These are the people who have given me their support, which is always much needed in following such a hard profession. I would like to say thank you very much to my dear wife Catherine; to Alastair Little, for his support from my early beginnings in England; to Annabel Wyatt, who organised the making of this book; to Ramon Pajares and the Inn on the Park Hotel, without whom this book would not have been possible, and to Norma MacMillan for her patience and invaluable help in the writing.